CALLED TO LEAD

LEADERSHIP DEVELOPMENT IN A SMALL COMMUNITY CONTEXT

3

Group Development

SUZANNE GOLAS, CSJP

PAULIST PRESS

New York / Mahwah

D1299732

The publisher gratefully acknowledges use of the following sources: *Guerrillas of Grace* by Ted Loder, ©1984 LuraMedia, Inc., San Diego, California. Excerpts from *The Emerging Parish* by Joseph Gremillion and Jim Castelli. Copyright © 1987 by James J. Castelli and Joseph Gremillion. Reprinted by permission of HarperCollins Publishers. Excerpts from *Women and Worship* by Sharon Neufer Emswiler and Thomas Neufer Emswiler. Copyright © 1974 by Sharon Neufer Emswiler and Thomas Neufer Emswiler. Reprinted by permission of HarperCollins Publishers. Excerpts from *More Than Words: Prayer and Ritual for Inclusive Communities* by Janet Schaffran and Pat Kozak. First edition © 1986 by Pat Kozak, CSJ, and Janet Schaffran, CDP; second revised edition © 1988. Reprinted by permission of The Crossroad Publishing Company. Excerpts from *Sadhana, A Way to God* by Anthony de Mello. Copyright ©1978 by Anthony de Mello. Used by permission of Doubleday, a division of Bantam Doubleday Dell Publishing Group, Inc. Excerpts from *The Leadership Book* by Charles J. Keating. First edition © 1978 by The Missionary Society of St. Paul the Apostle in the State of New York. Revised edition copyright © 1982 by Charles J. Keating. Reprinted by permission of Paulist Press. "A Meeting" is excerpted from *Miryam of Nazareth* by Ann Johnson. © Copyright 1984, Ave Maria Press, Notre Dame, IN 46556. Used with permission of the publisher.

Nihil Obstat: Rev. James M. Cafone, S.T.D.
Imprimatur: Most Rev. Theodore E. McCarrick, D.D., Archbishop of Newark

ISBN: 0-8091-9432-5

Published by Paulist Press
997 Macarthur Boulevard
Mahwah, New Jersey 07430

Printed and bound in the United States of America

CONTENTS

Book 3

FOREWORD

It is a great pleasure to introduce and recommend this timely and excellent contribution to the revitalization of the church. The return to the sources and reappropriation of what is best in our tradition which took place at the Second Vatican Council was so far-reaching in its implications for all of us that after several decades we are still slowly assimilating those implications. In the United States, the RENEW process has been a powerful instrument for that assimilation, and it has left many individuals and groups eager for further exploration of their Christian vocation. *Called To Lead* offers the opportunity to do that and more, with a program for guided group study, reflection, and prayer on the themes of scripture, church, sacramental life, lay spirituality, personal prayer, and community building at the grass-roots level—all through a process steeped in and empowered by the small group model.

Initiatives of this type have arisen in many parts of the world in a variety of basic Christian communities. It is a kind of groundswell responding to the call and inspiration of the Second Vatican Council—from many parts of the world and from many cultures—adapted to the styles of spirituality and modes of expression proper to various traditions. In this we seem to be seeing a moment of opportunity for Christian faith and action, a time of special grace and empowerment. And for encouraging this, *Called To Lead* appears at the right moment as an apt and excellent instrument. Our highly urbanized and swiftly moving society—with its transient populations, its numerous but impersonal contacts among individuals, and its stressful schedules and demands— does not easily lend itself to spontaneous grass-roots groupings of believers for study and prayer and mutual support. To counteract other pressures in the lives of individuals and families, a prepared and structured program is most helpful, if not absolutely necessary, and such a program is offered here.

This is an excellent time for new beginnings. If not now, then when? If not with this program, then why not?

—Monika K. Hellwig

*To my parents, Stella and Peter,
who gave me my first experience
of a small Christian community*

AUTHOR'S ACKNOWLEDGMENTS

I wish to acknowledge and thank the many people who have been a part of *Called To Lead,* in particular:

Msgr. Tom Kleissler, who first envisioned and initiated the idea of an instrument for the formation of small community leaders and who designed the final transparencies.

Mary McGuinness, O.P., for her faith, gentle prodding, patient attentiveness to details, piloting of the sessions and designing of the initial and final transparencies.

Kay Furlani who, with Mary, piloted these sessions over a two-year period, designed the initial transparencies, and provided perceptive observations.

Rev. John Russell, O. Carm., for his insightful critique, wisdom, and guidance throughout the writing.

Small Christian community members from many parishes in the Archdiocese of Newark, N.J., who enthusiastically participated in and critiqued the pilot sessions—especially those from St. Peter, Belleville; St. Philomena, Livingston; St. Peter the Apostle, River Edge; Holy Family, Nutley; and Church of the Presentation, Upper Saddle River.

Members of the Sisters of St. Joseph of Peace, who have shown consistent interest in the project.

Julie Jones, for her typing and supportive skills which have made this book possible.

Donna Ciangio, O.P., for artistically executing the transparency designs.

Alice Yohe, S.S.J., for her choice of additional music selections.

Maria Maggi, editor at Paulist Press, for her encouragement, patience, and creative integration of all aspects of *Called To Lead.*

PREFACE

Effective leadership is necessary if small Christian communities are to realize their potential and become centers of life within the church and the world. All participants in these communities are responsible for their own growth and for encouraging the growth of other members in the group. Therefore, in a certain sense, all share in leadership.

Pope John Paul II, in his *Apostolic Exhortation on the Laity,* states:

> In the present circumstances the lay faithful have an ability to do very much and therefore ought to do very much toward the growth of an authentic ecclesial communion in their parishes...
>
> *Christifideles Laici* 27, 1988

However, there is a specific leadership role for those who serve as designated leaders of these communities. In addition to providing organizational assistance, these leaders can do much to create an atmosphere that is supportive and prayerful and that is conducive to a more profound understanding and appreciation of faith and, in particular, of the truths of the Catholic faith.

> The more we are formed and the more we feel the need to pursue and deepen our formation, still more will we be formed and rendered capable of forming others.
>
> *Christifideles Laici* 63, 1988

Called To Lead: Leadership Development in a Small Community Context is a process designed specifically for forming small community leaders. Developed as a companion program to *Small Christian Communities: A Vision of Hope* by Msgr. Thomas A. Kleissler, Margo A. LeBert, and Mary C. McGuinness, O.P., it provides both theological content and practical skills for the development of good pastoral leadership.

Called To Lead is meant to provide an opportunity for personal growth that will also enable leaders to fulfill their role more effectively. This leadership formation program utilizes the small group format as an important part of its process.

The goal of this program is to provide, in a small group setting, an experience in which leaders of small groups will grow in the following ways.

– *They will know and understand their Catholic faith more fully.*

The program presents some concepts of Catholic teaching that are central to the thinking of the Second Vatican Council. Thus, while these materials are not a compendium of the teaching of the church, they are focused on some beliefs that are important for the development of small communities within the life of the church, and, specifically, within parish life. It is important, too, that small communities develop with a focus on and commitment to a faith life that is sensitive to the wider church and world. So, for example, the formational importance of scripture, the nature of the church, the significance of the sacraments, the primacy of eucharist, and the basic call to holiness of life and to mission and ministry are some of the themes of the sessions.

– *Participants will grow in confidence and ease in discussing their faith, especially within the context of small groups.*

Participants in these sessions will deepen their understanding of faith concepts through discussion of Catholic tradition in view of contemporary life, through reflection on their particular life experiences especially in relationship to scripture and church tradition, and through sharing both this reflection and prayer. This process will take place within a small group and so enable participants to grow in their ability to discuss and share faith within such a context.

– Participants will more fully recognize the fundamental importance of the communal dimension of Christianity.

It is presumed that participants in this program have already enjoyed a positive experience within a small group. It is probably this positive experience that evokes their response to a call to leadership in a group. As persons progress in their involvement with small groups, they often become increasingly interested in reflecting on the nature, meaning, and purpose of community. Thus the concept of community becomes a natural entry point in formation sessions for those who are striving to become effective small Christian community leaders. Since these sessions are specifically directed toward such persons, the "umbrella" theme of community will run through the program.

– Participants will deepen their awareness of the presence and action of the Holy Spirit in their lives.

This program focuses on spiritual growth rather than on facility in group dynamics or organizational skills. While some sessions on basic group dynamics are included to aid group interaction, the majority of the sessions concentrate on developing an awareness of faith and the values of a Catholic commitment, and a sensitivity to how God is present and active through the Spirit—in our personal lives as well as in the life of the church and the wider community.

– Participants will increase their realization of the social responsibilities of their faith.

Both Christian spirituality and Christian community are marked by a sense of mission—a sense of being about the reign of God which is the call of the church. This program helps participants to understand the implications of the social dimensions of their faith and encourages a concept of community in which reconciliation, justice, and peace are key concerns. Such understanding and awareness prevent small groups from becoming comfortable enclaves of self-satisfaction and self-service.

AN OVERVIEW OF THE PROGRAM

Part 1	
Introductory session (Session 1)	
Scripture (Sessions 2-9)	BOOK 1
The Church (Sessions 10-12)	
The Sacraments (Sessions 13-19)	
Mission (Session 20)	
Spirituality (Sessions 21-22)	BOOK 2
Prayer (Sessions 23-24)	
Part 2	
Group Development	
(Sessions 25-34)	BOOK 3

The first part of this leadership program deals with topics of Christian faith that are especially relevant to the development of small Christian communities. The second part deals with some practical aspects of group development, some principles of group dynamics, and some useful skills for effective facilitation and pastoral leadership within the groups.

Part 1

After an introductory session, the first group of sessions (2-9) looks at the formation of scripture. For many small community participants, the sharing of discussion and prayer on the scriptures is a highlight of their involvement. Their love for the Bible can be enriched and deepened as they come to a fuller understanding of how God speaks through the word. A better appreciation of the background and development of the scriptures leads to an increased awareness of the dynamic vitality of God's word. A knowledge of the roles of the community, the sacred writers, and official church leaders in the formation and determination of scripture contributes to the realization of the Spirit-filled process through which the Bible came to be. The inspired scriptures are a source of life for individuals and, at the same time, are entrusted to the community of the church with the guidance of its leaders. Such an awareness can serve as a safeguard against a too privatistic, narrow, literal, and fundamentalist approach to the Bible.

The second group of sessions (10-12) helps participants to understand the nature of the church of which their small communities are a part. It is important that small communities and their members see their connectedness to the parish, the diocese, and the universal church. This realization facilitates a clearer understanding of the church as the sacrament of Jesus' presence in the world, a source of grace, and an instrument for the fulfillment of the mission of Jesus. A sense of the different roles in the church—that is, the roles of the laity, the clergy, the bishops, and the pope—increases an understanding of how, concretely, the church carries out its mandate.

The third block of sessions (13-19) focuses on the sacraments. Through the sacramental life of the church, Jesus draws close to his people and effects bonds of unity and love. These sessions address the history and development of the sacraments, their significance and efficacious nature, and their communal dimension.

Because of its centrality in the life of the church, eucharist is accorded extensive treatment in three (17-19) of the seven sections dealing with the sacraments. Eucharist is viewed in relationship to the exodus-covenant event, sacrifice, meal, the real presence, community, and mission.

A truly eucharistic community must be involved in the mission of Jesus. In Session 20, participants are encouraged to examine how, in the concrete circumstances of their own lives, they can more fully enter into Jesus' mission.

The last two sections of this part of the program concentrate on spirituality (Sessions 21-22) and prayer (Sessions 23-24). Spirituality is discussed as the efforts of a person to recognize, acknowledge, and respond to God's loving action in his or her life. In Christian spirituality the individual is involved in a personal relationship with Jesus Christ and lives in openness to the action of the Spirit in his or her life. Catholics are nurtured in their spiritual growth through the church's teachings, worship, sacraments, ministry, and witness in the world.

Participants are called to recognize the invitation to grow spiritually in their own lives. They will hopefully come to see how the movement of the Spirit and events of history have given rise to specific "spiritualities" in the church and how these spiritualities are tested on the basis of fundamental Catholic teaching on the revelation of God in Jesus. Insights will be gleaned as they examine some trends in spirituality which have become prevalent since Vatican II.

The sessions on prayer should help participants to understand the nature and importance of prayer. An emphasis on various prayer styles enables them to experience different prayer forms. Practical suggestions are offered for deepening prayer life.

Part 2

In the second part of this leadership program participants are assisted in understanding the evolution (Session 25) and stages of development (Session 26) in small groups. Such understanding prepares them for the dynamics that frequently occur as groups form and continue to meet and solidify.

The sessions on communication (27-30) employ practical exercises that emphasize the skills of listening, giving feedback, and resolving conflict. Decision making through a consensus process is presented (Session 31) as a means for nurturing the unity, creativity, and strength of the group.

Additional tips are suggested in Session 32 for those who have designated leadership responsibilities specifically in small Christian communities. Participants are also asked to assess their own strengths and weaknesses in leading small groups and are helped in developing confidence in areas in which they feel weak (Session 33).

The last session (34) is a reflection on "being called," and participants are encouraged to see their leadership responsibilities as a call from God.

In the *Apostolic Exhortation on the Laity,* John Paul II states:

> ...re-evangelization is directed not only to individual persons, but also to entire portions of populations in the variety of their situations, surroundings and cultures. Its purpose is the formation of mature ecclesial communities in which the faith might radiate and fulfill the basic meaning of adherence to the person of Christ and his Gospel, of an encounter and sacramental communion with him, and of an existence lived in charity and in service. The lay faithful have their part to fulfill in the formation of these ecclesial communities..."

Christifideles Laici 34

It is hoped that these sessions of *Called To Lead* will help the faithful meet this challenge.

INTRODUCTION AND SUGGESTIONS FOR IMPLEMENTATION

Called To Lead has been developed specifically for leaders of small groups and small Christian communities.

Some fundamental concepts of the Catholic faith are presented simply and clearly in a formation process that utilizes a small group context. Participation and the introduction of group members to discussion and to the sharing of experience, prayer, and reflection are a crucial part of the process.

The information presented is basic, yet developed to enable participants to become more knowledgeable and skilled in sharing some of the most profound beliefs of our faith.

Called To Lead is geared for leaders or facilitators of small groups. However, once experienced by leaders it could easily be duplicated within the groups themselves and would thus be an enriching experience shared by leaders and their groups. It would also be an excellent formation process for members of core communities and other groups/teams within parishes.

While *Called To Lead* is primarily for leaders of ongoing small groups/communities, it can be used with other groups if those groups value the development of community. For example, this process could benefit a pastoral council and parish committees and other groups that function within a communal context. The entire process can be adopted by a diocese or a parish for developing leaders and/or strengthening those already in leadership roles. The "Presentation" materials have also been successfully used by those preparing talks for Cursillo, the catechumenate, parish missions and retreats.

Format of This Leader's Manual

For the convenience of the leaders, this manual contains the text not only of the Leader's Manual but also of the Workbook. The text which is cen-
tered and in larger type is the only text found in the Workbook. The smaller type which is set in two columns indicates text found only in the Leader's Manual.

	Sequence of Sessions	
	PART 1	
	Topic	*No. of Sessions*
	Introduction	1
Block 1	Scripture	8
Block 2	Church	3
Block 3	Sacraments	4
Block 4	Eucharist / Mission	3
Block 5	Mission	1
Block 6	Spirituality	2
Block 7	Prayer	2
	PART 2	
Block 8	Group Development	10

Scheduling

This program is developmental. However, the order of the blocks can be changed to meet local needs. In any reordering, two recommendations should be seriously considered:

1. Maintain the order of the sessions within each block since change would disrupt the development of important concepts.

2. Begin the program with the introduction and the block of eight sessions on scripture, since this block is foundational.

Part 2 could precede Part 1 if such an order meets a group's needs. Also, sessions of Part 2 could be combined with blocks of Part 1.

The program allows for wide flexibility in scheduling. What follows are two suggested formats based on the sequence of the sessions as outlined above:

1. Implementation over Two Years

Fall	6 sessions (first year)
	5 sessions (second year)
Winter	6 sessions (first year)
	5 sessions (second year)
Spring/Summer	7 sessions (first year)
	5 sessions (second year)

2. Implementation over Three Years

Fall	5 sessions (first year)
	4 sessions (second year)
	2 sessions (third year)
Winter	4 sessions (first year)
	3 sessions (second year)
	5 sessions (third year)
Spring/Summer	3 sessions (first year)
	3 sessions (second year)
	5 sessions (third year)

Participation

Called To Lead is implemented utilizing the context of small groups. Group members can be involved in the actual preparation and implementation of the program.

For example, individual group members can prepare and lead the prayer segments, facilitate the group experiences and responses, and provide hospitality and help create a suitable environment.

The presentations may be given by a person who has some background in church teaching and who can also develop the themes with the integration of personal experience. However, piloting of these materials and experimentation have shown that, sometimes, there are participants in the group who, given the materials in advance, can make the presentation either as individuals or in a team of two. Once having experienced the program, many participants are able to duplicate it for other groups.

Use of Transparencies

The transparency designs to be used with *Called To Lead* are available from the International Office of RENEW, 1232 George Street, Plainfield, NJ 07062, 1-908-769-5400. They are intended as a valuable visual teaching instrument for the presenter. They are meant to be used primarily as tools for conveying some of the key concepts within the presentation material as opposed to a mini capsulized presentation in themselves. Therefore, they do not tell the story on their own.

Presenters are encouraged to make transparencies from these designs on a duplicating machine, and to supplement them as they choose their own unique designs in order to make the presentation their own as much as possible.

Other forms of visual aids can also be very valuable. For example, for Session 1 a slide show that conveys the various ways we come to experience God is very effective. To do this with local scenes as well as those from around the world (if available) could prove quite meaningful to participants.

Further Suggestions and Recommendations

Following are some further suggestions and recommendations that will contribute to the effectiveness of the sessions:

- *Called To Lead*, because it utilizes a small group context, presumes the development of an increasing sense of community within the group. At the first session, participants are placed in small groups of six to ten members. Unless otherwise stipulated in the individual sessions, participants should experience the entire program with the same members of this small group. The leader can emphasize the importance of each member's presence and participation within this small group. This would also be a good time to urge participants to attend the sessions regularly, since the learning and growth of the small group of which they are a part will depend on the ongoing presence of each member.

Practical considerations can contribute to the functioning of these groups. For example, the arrangement of the groups can be such that members of each group can easily hear one another and not be distracted by the conversations of other groups.

– The leader ought to be familiar with the entire program and anticipate the requirements of the next session. Some sessions include assignments for the following week. Some sessions require that each participant have a Bible.

– In general, it is important to adhere to the time schedule since the effectiveness of each session is dependent on the experience of all the segments of the session.

– The "Presentation" materials include basic information for the presentation. (Remember that master copies for transparencies for each session are available from the International Office of RENEW.) The presenter will want to "flesh out" the presentation by incorporating personal experience and additional information relative to the specific area and group. In many of the sessions, it will also be helpful if the presenter, while being faithful to the schedule, still allows some time for questions and comments.

– Environment is important. This is especially true for the "Prayer" segments. Use of music, candles, flowers, an enthroned Bible, etc., can do wonders in creating an atmosphere conducive to prayer and reflection. While the "Music Resources" list at the end of the Leader's Manual provides suggestions for recorded music, live music (for example, a guitarist or flutist) is usually much more effective.

– Finally, it is helpful to remember that attention to detail and involvement of participants can contribute mightily to the successful implementation of *Called To Lead*.

INTRODUCTION TO THE WORKBOOK

Welcome to *Called To Lead,* a process that will enable you to grow in your leadership skills in the following ways:

- as you come to know and understand your Catholic faith more fully;
- as you grow in confidence and ease in discussing your faith, especially within the context of a small group;
- as you recognize more fully the fundamental importance of the communal dimension of Christianity;
- as you deepen your awareness of the presence and action of the Holy Spirit in your life; and
- as you increase your realization of the social responsibilities of your faith.

These are significant goals, but, most definitely, goals worth achieving. You are invited to make the investment of time and to be guided by the sense of commitment. By giving of your time and yourself, you will make your *Called To Lead* experience a rich and fruitful one.

WHAT HAPPENS IN A SMALL CHRISTIAN COMMUNITY?

SAMPLE SCHEDULE

Welcome/Presentation of Aims	5 min.
Opening Prayer	5 min.
Presentation	20 min.
Group Experience	55 min.
Break	5 min.
Scripture Sharing	20 min.
Building Understanding	5 min.
Closing Prayer	5 min.

PREPARATION

With the beginning of this new unit, it is hoped that participants already have their Workbooks for these 10 sessions. Again, the seats should be arranged as has become customary for the participants. The Bible should be positioned prominently, opened to the reading from Revelation which will be read during the Opening Prayer.

Ask for a volunteer to prepare this reading. Point out that the verses are not in sequence.

Also, set up a record player, cassette player, or CD player with instrumental music which will continue to play softly throughout the Opening Prayer.

AIMS

To provide an opportunity—through group experience, discussion, presentation of information, and reflection—for participants to grow in their understanding and appreciation of the following:

- important elements in the development of small Christian communities;
- the relational and task aspects of community;
- the importance of awareness of the difference between task and relationship in the dynamics of community.

To provide an opportunity for participants to practice skills in the following:

- reaching consensus;
- identifying task and relational dynamics within group discussion.

WELCOME/PRESENTATION OF AIMS (5 min.)

OPENING PRAYER (5 min.)

(Depending on the size of the group, you may decide that it is better for all to speak their names together rather than individually.)

Call to Remember

Leader: Let us pause in our busy lives and remember that God is with us.

(brief pause)

Reading (Revelation 3:12, 5)

Reader: A reading from the book of Revelation.

Leader: We pray at this moment that our names may never be erased from the book of the living. With this hope in our hearts, let us individually [or in unison, if deemed appropriate] present ourselves to God, with our strengths and weaknesses, by simply saying our name aloud.

(If names are spoken individually, the leader may wish to begin.)

Concluding Prayer

Leader: God, our creator, we gather ourselves together under the one name—Christian. We ask that as individuals and as a community we may become ever more true to our name—true to the name of Jesus Christ, your Son. Amen.

PRESENTATION OUTLINE

I. Some common characteristics are often found in small Christian communities. Some of these characteristics are the following:
    A. prayer
    B. sharing
    C. mutual support
    D. learning
    E. mission

II. All groups are involved in two functions—the task function and the relationship function.
    A. The nature of the group determines which function is emphasized.
    B. In a healthy small Christian community, tasks and relationships are kept in a dynamic balance.
    C. Good leaders are concerned about "relation skills" and "task skills."
    D. Good leaders know that their role is to recognize the talents of others and to encourage different members of the community to assume responsibility for the task and relation functions within the group.
    E. The following are examples of specific relation functions within a group:
        1. encouraging
        2. harmonizing
        3. compromising
        4. gatekeeping
        5. expressing feelings
        6. setting standards
    F. The following are examples of specific task functions within a group:
        1. initiating
        2. seeking information or opinions
        3. supporting
        4. clarifying
        5. summarizing
        6. consensus testing

PRESENTATION (25 min.)

Important Elements in the Development of Small Christian Communities

In parishes, there are usually many groups which exist for a variety of good reasons. Although these groups may have a communal aspect, most do not cultivate self-consciously the dynamics which foster Christian community. Yet, increasingly, people are looking for an experience of true community. Observation of the many small Christian communities that are appearing throughout the church seems to indicate that there are certain common elements that are found in many of these communities.

Let's consider some of these important components in the development of groups, which are indeed small Christian communities:

Prayer

The element of prayer emphasizes the centrality of God's active presence in the life of each member of the small Christian community and in the life of the community itself. As the group prays together, there can be a keen sense of that presence and a greater willingness to acknowledge dependence on God and on one another.

Sharing

Small Christian communities talk freely and openly about God and about life and experiences, reflecting on these experiences in the light of scripture and tradition. Often this sharing results in more profound insights and a strengthening of the belief of others in the community.

Mutual Support

In a society in which gospel values are all too frequently ridiculed and rejected, the believer needs a community that is supportive of these values. The small Christian community encourages fidelity to the gospel and also challenges itself and its members to a more profound and authentic commitment to Christian living.

Learning

Small Christian communities are part of the wider church. These communities and their members are called to an ever fuller knowledge and understanding of the gospel, of the Catholic Church and its teaching on faith and morals, and of the relationship of that teaching to the circumstances and issues of their lives.

Mission

Authentic Christian communities are, like Jesus, committed to a life of loving service, a life involved in the mission of Jesus—a mission that has been understood and articulated by the church. As a group and through its individual members, the community will work for compassion, justice, reconciliation, and peace within the group, in the family, in the workplace, in the neighborhood, and within the wider society. The community and its members will strive for a greater awareness of and reverence for the interrelatedness of all creation. Thus each community can fulfill the biblical and ecclesial call to servant leadership.

The Task and Relational Aspects of Community Life

All of us are members of many different groups. All of these groups are involved in two functions—the task function and the relationship function. The nature of a group determines which function is emphasized. For example, while executing certain tasks is necessary for a family's survival, the actual relationships between the members are at the core of the meaning of family. Thus, in healthy families, there is an emphasis on sustaining, developing, and nurturing those relationships. In contrast, in a group like an adult education class, while some relating may be helpful and necessary, the emphasis is usually on the task of learning.

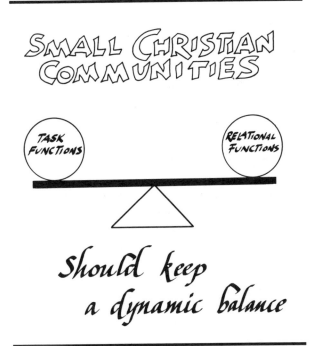

Small Christian Communities

TASK FUNCTIONS

RELATIONAL FUNCTIONS

Should keep a dynamic balance

In a healthy small Christian community, tasks and relationships are kept in a dynamic balance. If the community focuses excessively on the task, the group may keep to its schedule, do the scripture sharing, "get the prayer in," or accomplish a service project, but there may be minimal individual ownership or involvement. On the other hand, if the focus is excessively on relationship, everyone may feel good for a while. Eventually, however, confusion, frustration, and boredom will set in.

Most people have a natural inclination toward one function or another. A particular group may also have a bias. It is the role of all the members of the community and, especially of the leader or facilitator, to be attentive to achieving an equilibrium between relationship and task. Such an effort requires a conscious awareness of the two functions and a common understanding of the ideal for which the community is striving.

While small Christian communities will try to balance the two, some parish groups may opt to emphasize task over relationship or relationship over task. The very nature of the group may call for such an option.

However, if the group is to have some sense of community, some attention must be given to both functions. Even in parish groups it is helpful for members to discuss expectations and to agree on the place of prayer, reflection, work, and socializing in their group and to become more adept at both "task skills" and "relation skills."

Good community leaders are concerned about "relation skills" which help the members to interact, to communicate, and to support and challenge one another effectively. They are also concerned about "task skills" of organization, planning, and evaluating. They recognize that their role is not to exercise all these skills (which would be impossible, since they could not possess them all), but rather to recognize the talents of others and to encourage different members of the community to assume responsibility for the task and relation functions. Leadership within a small Christian community is primarily a matter of facilitating a collaborative process among the members.

Examples of Specific Relation Functions

What follows are examples of specific relation functions that can be helpful in maintaining and increasing effective interaction within groups. All members of the community have responsibility for exercising relational skills.

Encouraging—being friendly, warm, and responsive to others; accepting and affirming their contributions; asking to hear more about their ideas and feelings on a subject.

Harmonizing—attempting to reconcile disagreements among others; facilitating the exploration of the differences and the similarities in ideas and recognizing what is of value in both.

Compromising—being willing to modify one's opinions when possible; admitting mistakes; adjusting oneself to the pace of the group.

Gatekeeping—facilitating the participation of others, especially those who are less vocal; suggesting ways that the opinions and feelings of all might be expressed, that is, "opening the gate" to the fuller use of the group's resources.

Expressing feelings—sharing one's own feelings or the feelings one senses in the group; expressing pleasure and satisfaction in being and working with the group; expressing tension felt in the group.

Setting standards—testing whether the group is satisfied with its procedures and progress; challenging the group to use time or structures better; suggesting ways of evaluating the human interaction in the group.

Examples of Specific Task Functions

What follows are examples of specific task functions that can be helpful in accomplishing particular work within a group. While all members of the group are responsible for relational functions, different task functions may be accomplished by different members of the group, depending on who has various skills.

Initiating—suggesting ways to proceed; proposing ideas for solving a problem or tackling a task.

Seeking information or opinions—asking for or giving facts, information, ideas, opinions, feelings, feedback, or clarification of suggestions.

Supporting—building on the ideas of another/others; elaborating on the thoughts of another.

Clarifying—interpreting ideas or suggestions; clearing up confusion; defining terms, indicating alternatives; presenting examples; developing meanings.

Summarizing—digesting the discussion of the group; sharing with the group members what you hear them saying; pulling together related ideas.

Consensus testing—asking if a group is nearing a decision; offering a decision or a conclusion for the group to accept or reject.

"Specific Relation Functions" and
"Specific Task Functions"
Adapted from *The Leadership Book*
by Charles J. Keating
Paulist Press, Mahwah, NJ

GROUP EXPERIENCE (55 min.)

To help ensure the effectiveness of this Group Experience, ask the participants to form groups of 6 to 8.

Part 1 (30 min.)

Tell the participants that this Group Experience will have two parts. In the first part, there will be about 10 minutes of silence to allow them to read Reflection Sheet #22 on pages 5-6 of their Workbooks.

Reading of Reflection Sheet #22

After 10 minutes or so, explain to the participants that they will have the next 15 minutes to reach an agreement within their group on the two questions at the end of Reflection Sheet #22. Though an accord may not be easy to achieve, tell the participants that they should make every effort to arrive at answers that, at a minimum, all the group members can live with.

Group Discussion

Once the discussions are finished, take a quick survey to see what answers the group arrived at and why.

Part 2 (25 min.)

Explain to the participants that while they were attempting to agree on their answers, each of them made contributions and played roles—whether or not they were conscious of these actions. Ask them to recall their group discussion as they read Reflection Sheets #23 and #24 on pages 7-8 and 9-10, respectively, of their Workbooks, and to identify the particular contributions that they and other members in their group made.

Reading of Reflection Sheets #23 and #24

After 5 minutes or so, ask the participants to describe their own specific contributions or roles or those of other group members. You may wish to add your own observations, but do so only after all the participants have shared their ideas.

Group Discussion

You could conclude this segment by reminding the participants of the importance and value of being more sensitive to "task" and "relationship" in their groups and communities.

BREAK (5 min.)

SCRIPTURE SHARING (20 min.)

Ask for a volunteer to read the following passage aloud.

Reading (John 17:20-26)

Question for Discussion

Describe a concrete example in which you experienced a deep sense of unity with other believers. What contributed to this experience of community?

BUILDING UNDERSTANDING (5 min.)

Ask the participants to review the relation functions and task functions considered during this session and evaluate themselves as objectively as possible in relation to both types of functions. Have them reflect on what their strengths and weaknesses are and how they might improve their skills.

CLOSING PRAYER (5 min.)

Leader: We have been involved in much discussion in the past two hours. Let us now spend a few short moments in silence together, thanking God for the insights and inspirations we've had during this time.

(brief period of silence)

Leader: Let us close by joining hands and singing the Our Father.

REFLECTION SHEET #22

Important Elements in the Development of Small Christian Communities

Prayer

The element of prayer emphasizes the centrality of God's active presence in the life of each member of the small Christian community and in the life of the community itself. As the group prays together, there can be a keen sense of that presence and a greater willingness to acknowledge dependence on God and on one another.

Sharing

Small Christian communities talk freely and openly about God and about life and experiences, reflecting on these experiences in the light of scripture and tradition. Often this sharing results in more profound insights and a strengthening of the belief of others in the community.

Mutual Support

In a society in which gospel values are all too frequently ridiculed and rejected, the believer needs a community that is supportive of these values. The small Christian community encourages fidelity to the gospel and also challenges itself and its members to a more profound and authentic commitment to Christian living.

Learning

Small Christian communities are part of the wider church. These communities and their members are called to an ever fuller knowledge and understanding of the gospel, of the Catholic Church and its teaching on faith and morals, and of the relationship of that teaching to the circumstances and issues of their lives.

Mission

Authentic Christian communities are, like Jesus, committed to a life of loving service, a life involved in the mission of Jesus—a mission that has been understood and articulated by the church. As a group and through its individual members, the community will work for compassion, justice, reconciliation, and peace within the group, in the family, in the workplace, in the neighborhood, and within the wider society. The community and its members will strive for a greater awareness of and reverence for the interrelatedness of all creation. Thus each community can fulfill the biblical and ecclesial call to servant leadership.

Questions for Discussion

Which element is easiest to develop and continue in a small community?

Which element is most difficult to develop and continue in a small community?

REFLECTION SHEET #23

Examples of Specific Relation Functions

What follows are examples of specific relation functions that can be helpful in maintaining and increasing effective interaction within groups. All members of the community have responsibility for exercising relational skills.

Encouraging—being friendly, warm, and responsive to others; accepting and affirming their contributions; asking to hear more about their ideas and feelings on a subject.

Harmonizing—attempting to reconcile disagreements among others; facilitating the exploration of the differences and the similarities in ideas and recognizing what is of value in both.

Compromising—being willing to modify one's opinions when possible; admitting mistakes; adjusting oneself to the pace of the group.

Gatekeeping—facilitating the participation of others, especially those who are less vocal; suggesting ways that the opinions and feelings of all might be expressed, that is, "opening the gate" to the fuller use of the group's resources.

Expressing feelings—sharing one's own feelings or the feelings one senses in the group; expressing pleasure and satisfaction in being and working with the group; expressing tension felt in the group.

Setting standards—testing whether the group is satisfied with its procedures and progress; challenging the group to use time or structures better; suggesting ways of evaluating the human interaction in the group.

Adapted from *The Leadership Book*
by Charles J. Keating
Paulist Press, Mahwah, NJ

REFLECTION SHEET #24

Examples of Specific Task Functions

What follows are examples of specific task functions that can be helpful in accomplishing particular work within a group. While all members of the group are responsible for relational functions, different task functions may be accomplished by different members of the group, depending on who has various skills.

Initiating—suggesting ways to proceed; proposing ideas for solving a problem or tackling a task.

Seeking information or opinions—asking for or giving facts, information, ideas, opinions, feelings, feedback, or clarification of suggestions.

Supporting—building on the ideas of another/others; elaborating on the thoughts of another.

Clarifying—interpreting ideas or suggestions; clearing up confusion; defining terms; indicating alternatives; presenting examples; developing meanings.

Summarizing—digesting the discussion of the group; sharing with the group members what you hear them saying; pulling together related ideas.

Consensus testing—asking if a group is nearing a decision; offering a decision or a conclusion for the group to accept or reject.

Adapted from *The Leadership Book*
by Charles J. Keating
Paulist Press, Mahwah, NJ

STAGES IN THE DEVELOPMENT OF A GROUP

SAMPLE SCHEDULE

Welcome/Presentation of Aim	5 min.
Opening Prayer	10 min.
Presentation	20 min.
Group Experience	50 min.
Break	5 min.
Scripture Sharing	20 min.
Building Understanding	5 min.
Closing Prayer	5 min.

PREPARATION

The Bible should be positioned prominently and opened to the first of the passages from the gospel of John that will be read during the Scripture Sharing segment.

Ask for two volunteers to prepare the two readings for the Opening Prayer.

You will need to provide large sheets of newsprint, markers, and masking tape for the Group Experience segment.

AIM

To provide an opportunity—through discussion, reflection, prayer, presentation of information, and scripture sharing—for participants to grow in their understanding and appreciation of the following:

-   a group's stages of development;
-   the leadership tasks needed for each stage.

WELCOME/PRESENTATION OF AIM (5 min.)

OPENING PRAYER (10 min.)

Leader: Let us begin this session by listening to a reading by author M. Scott Peck and a quotation from St. Therese of Lisieux.

Reader 1: M. Scott Peck writes, "It is true that we are called to wholeness. But the reality is that we can never be completely whole in and of ourselves. We cannot be all things to ourselves and to others. We cannot be perfect. We cannot be doctors, lawyers, stockbrokers, farmers, politicians, stonemasons, and theologians, all rolled into one. It is true that we are called to power. Yet the reality is that there is a point beyond which our sense of self-determination not only becomes inaccurate and prideful but increasingly self-defeating. It is true that we are created to be individually unique. Yet the reality is that we are inevitably social creatures who desperately need each other not merely for sustenance, not merely for company, but for any meaning to our lives whatsoever. These, then, are the paradoxical seeds from which community can grow."

From *The Different Drum*
Simon and Schuster
New York, NY, pp. 54-55

Reader 2: St. Therese said, "I feel within me other vocations. I feel the vocation of . . . the priest, the apostle, the doctor, the martyr. . . . I understood that love comprised all vocations, that love was everything, that it embraced all times and places . . . in a word, that it was eternal! Then in the excess of my delirious joy, I cried out: O Jesus, my Love. . . my vocation, at last I have found it. . . . My vocation is love!"

From *The Story of a Soul*
translated by John Clarke, O.C.D.
Institute of Carmelite Studies
Washington, D.C., 1976, pp. 192, 194

(Invite participants to name a community they wish
to pray for and then begin by naming a community.
Pause for names.)

Leader: We thank you, O loving God, for these communities in our lives.

PRESENTATION OUTLINE

I.   All groups go through stages of development.
   A.   Both awareness and understanding of the stages of group development are important not only for groups but also for their leaders.
      1.   Such awareness and understanding help participants to be more realistic in their expectations.
      2.   Such awareness and understanding help participants to be more comfortable with the dynamics which accompany each stage.
      3.   Such awareness and understanding help a group to move from one stage to another more easily.
   B.   Stages are a helpful guide, but not a magic formula.
      1.   Stages may overlap, although one stage is usually dominant.
      2.   Groups can regress to an earlier stage or become fixated in one stage.
      3.   A group may skip a stage and return to it at a later date.
      4.   Different stages may occur during the course of a meeting as well as over the lifetime of the group.

II. A model of group development which is especially helpful to small Christian communities includes the following five stages:
   A.   The Polite Stage
   B.   The Why We're Here Stage
   C.   The Bid for Power Stage
   D.   The Constructive Stage
   E.   The Esprit Stage

SMALL CHRISTIAN COMMUNITY

LEADERS

SHOULD KNOW
COMMUNITY STAGES
OF DEVELOPMENT

HELP MEMBERS TO
UNDERSTAND STAGES

○ ENABLES REALISTIC EXPECTATIONS

○ FACILITATES COMFORT WITH
VARIOUS DYNAMICS

Stages of Group Development

All groups go through stages of development. It is important for leaders to be aware of these stages and to help group members to understand the stages. Such awareness and understanding enable the group to be more realistic in its expectations, to be more comfortable with the dynamics which accompany the various stages, and to move from one stage to another more easily.

It is important to remember, however, that describing stages is indeed helpful, but it does not provide a magic formula. All groups are different; the individuals making up the group are different. Often stages overlap, although one stage is usually dominant. Groups can regress to an earlier stage or become fixated in one stage. A group may skip a stage and return to it at a later date. Different stages may occur during the course of a meeting as well as over the lifetime of the group.

Different models have been developed to name and describe the stages of group development. A model

which is especially helpful in discussing small Christian communities is called Cog's Ladder. This model has five stages which are called The Polite Stage, The Why We're Here Stage, The Bid for Power Stage, The Constructive Stage, and The Esprit Stage.

Let's consider these five stages as described in Reflection Sheet #25 on pages 17-20 of the Workbook.

The Polite Stage

In this stage, people become acquainted and experience first impressions. Often, at the first meeting of a group, most members tend to feel inadequate and try to hide their feelings of inadequacy. There is a high priority on wanting to be liked. People are cautious about revealing themselves and talk tends to be superficial chatter. There usually is great dependency on the group leader. There is an anxiety which diminishes as people come to know one another better. As people interact, they slowly drop their guards and persons are gradually seen as unique individuals with differences as well as similarities.

The Why We're Here Stage

In this stage, the group is trying to define its goals and purposes. Those who gather to form a small Christian community or group certainly know in some general sense that the group will focus on gospel values. They may be quite unsure as to what this might concretely mean. Even if the leader has a clearer understanding of the reason for the group, each group member will have to go through some process of internalizing the definition and purpose of the group. Consciously or unconsciously, each member will be focusing on questions including: "Who are these people?" "Do I belong here?" "How will this group meet my personal needs?" "Why do they need me; what do I have to contribute?" "Do I agree with the basic purpose of this group?" There may be hidden agendas—that is, individual plans to use the group for one's own purposes. These may be unconscious plans. Cliques may begin to develop. Group identity is still low. The nature and importance of the group are still vague and expectations are still uncertain. Time is needed for the group to clarify, discuss, and internalize the purpose, ground rules, and boundaries of the group.

The Bid for Power Stage

There is sometimes a reluctance to recognize the existence of power dynamics and conflict within Christian communities. However, since these are normal developments within all groups, it is unrealistic to think that such dynamics will be avoided in small Christian communities. Power dynamics and conflict are not only not bad, they are necessary if a group is to mature.

In this stage, individuals may, consciously or unconsciously, question, "How much can I influence this group?" "How much will the group and its individual members influence me?" "How much do I want to be influenced?" "Who's really important in this group?" People are concerned that they are not wasting their time and energy and that they will have some control over what happens within the group. Different individuals may surface different, and seemingly contradictory, needs and values. In a small Christian community the group and individuals can often address these questions within a common vision of community that comes from the shared reflection on scripture and the shared prayer that are a regular part of the life of the community.

It is important that, in some way, unresolved conflict issues are surfaced and dealt with directly or they will continue to smolder below the surface and the group will not be able to move with surety to the next stage.

The Constructive Stage

In this stage, there is a greater possibility for attitudinal changes. Group members really listen to one another and are open to different opinions and ideas. They share at a deeper level, trusting in the acceptance of the group. Creative thinking is encouraged and critiqued in a spirit of "give and take." There is less reluctance to challenge one another. Capitalizing on the various strengths and skills of its members, the group arrives at accurate conclusions and creative decisions. Decisions are implemented by everyone since the whole group has "ownership," that is, each person feels that his or her opinion has been heard and respected. Since there is a sense of group identity, it can be difficult to introduce new members into the group at this point. Just as the group had to progress through the three earlier stages in order to arrive at the Constructive stage, so a new member will have to experience the same process before arriving at this point of cohesiveness.

The Esprit Stage

At this point, the group experiences a high spirit of unity and group morale. There is intense group loyalty and great pleasure in being together. Emotional ties are strong and there is a high level of trust. Members look forward to sharing joys and sorrows with one another and can depend on the group for support, affirmation, and affection.

Members could begin to experience a reluctance to disturb the harmony of the group and could "backslide" to former stages as they begin to avoid conflict and any dynamic that resembles confrontation. Nurturing one another and the group could become a preoccupation. Furthermore, since the group identity is so strong and the sense of unity so intense, the introduction of new members can be disturbing for everyone unless the group consciously accepts the adjustments that will be necessary for a new person to be integrated into the group.

Adapted from
The Leadership Book
by Charles J. Keating
Paulist Press, Mahwah, NJ

GROUP EXPERIENCE (50 min.)

Ask the participants to turn to Reflection Sheet #26 on pages 21-22 of their Workbooks. Before the participants complete the Reflection Sheet, ask them to re-read the descriptions of each stage of group development given on Reflection Sheet #25, think of experiences they have had in groups, and then jot down how they think a leader can help a group's progress in each of the five stages listed. Tell the participants that they will have 10 minutes of silence to complete the Reflection Sheet.

Completion of Reflection Sheet #26

Distribute newsprint and markers to each group.

Ask each group to develop a combined list of leadership tasks for each stage of group development, using the following process. For each stage, first have each group member share his/her personal list of tasks. Next, have the group as a whole decide upon the important leadership tasks. Then, on the newsprint, itemize the tasks beneath each stage. Tell the participants that they will have 25 minutes to complete this process.

After 25 minutes have passed, have each group display its list by taping it where it is in full view for all participants to see. Encourage participants to seek explanation or clarification from other groups as necessary. You too may need to have some things explained or clarified.

If certain things haven't been considered once all discussion seems exhausted, it may be necessary for you to add to the posted lists, using the suggestions listed below.

Tell the participants that future sessions will help them develop skills needed for the various stages of group development.

You should allow approximately 15 minutes for the last part of this segment. If there are many groups sharing and clarifying their lists, however, you may wish to allow more time.

**Some Leader's Tasks in the
Stages of Group Development**

Polite Stage:

1. Create a "friendly" climate.
   - chairs in circle
   - refreshments (possibly in the beginning for the first session rather than at a break)
   - call people by name
   - use name tags to help people get to know names

2. Facilitate introductions.
   - informally introduce people who don't know one another as they arrive
   - formally go around the circle and have people introduce themselves and give some background

3. Establish some ground rules.
   - establish beginning and ending times; encourage promptness; assure participants that sessions will end on time
   - ask people to call if they will be absent
   - confirm meeting dates

Why We're Here Stage:

1. Elicit expectations and hopes.

2. Clarify purpose and direction of group as a small Christian community concerned with gospel values.

3. Encourage common understanding of purpose and direction of group.

Bid for Power Stage:

1. Provide encouragement, harmonizing, and compromise.

2. Encourage faithfulness to shared reflection on the gospels and shared prayer.

3. Help individuals name their gifts.

4. Affirm the unique value of each person.

5. Point out the common desire to live lives more faithful to Christ and to build Christian community.

6. Bring conflict to the fore and deal with it.

7. Be firm about non-negotiables and flexible about other things.

8. Avoid being defensive.

Constructive Stage:

1. Listen carefully.

2. Ask constructive questions.

3. Help in clarifying and summarizing.

4. Trust the group.

5. Affirm talents, skills, and initiative.

6. Encourage members to take on further responsibilities in the group.

Esprit Stage:

1. Make sure physical needs of the group are tended to (agenda, meeting place, materials, etc.).

2. Be available to the group and its members.

3. Beware of tendencies to regress to prior stages.

4. Engage the group in outreach and service beyond themselves to avoid preoccupation with nurturing one another and the group.

5. Help the group recognize the discomfort and adjustment needed when a newcomer joins.

BREAK (5 min.)

SCRIPTURE SHARING (20 min.)

Ask for two volunteers to read the following passages aloud.

Reading 1 (John 15:9-10, 12-13)

Reading 2 (John 17:20-23)

Ask participants to reflect quietly on the following question for a few moments before they respond.

Question for Discussion

Striving for the unity that is Christian community often requires great effort and a type of laying down of one's life. Describe an experience in your life in which there was an especially hard struggle to build an authentic Christian community. Perhaps it was your family or a parish group. In what ways did members of the group have to "lay down their lives" for the community?

BUILDING UNDERSTANDING (5 min.)

Ask the participants to review the stages in group development and reflect on what particular stage proved most challenging to them in their own small group and why.

CLOSING PRAYER (5 min.)

Designate which groups will pray the verses indicated with a "1." and which will pray the verses indicated with a "2."

Leader: Let us pray together.

1. Wondrous Worker of Wonders,
    I praise you
    not alone for what has been,
    or for what is,
    but for what is yet to be,
    for you are gracious beyond all telling of it.

2. I praise you
    that out of the turbulence of my life
    a kingdom is coming,
    is being shaped even now
    out of my slivers of loving,
    my bits of trusting,
    my sprigs of hoping,
    my tootles of laughing,
    my drips of crying,
    my smidgens of worshipping;
    that out of my songs and struggles,
    out of my griefs and triumphs,
    I am gathered up and saved,
    for you are gracious beyond all telling of it.

1. I praise you
    that you turn me loose
    to go with you to the edge of now and maybe,
    to welcome the new,
    to see my possibilities,
    to accept my limits,
    and yet begin living to the limit
    of passion and compassion
    until,
    released by joy,
    I uncurl to other people
    and to your kingdom coming,
    for you are gracious beyond all telling of it.

"I Praise You for What Is Yet To Be"
From *Guerrillas of Grace*
by Ted Loder
LuraMedia, San Diego, CA, 1984

REFLECTION SHEET #25

Stages in the Development of a Group

Different models have been developed to name and describe the stages of group development. A model which is especially help-ful in discussing small Christian communities is called Cog's Ladder. This model has five stages which are called The Polite Stage, The Why We're Here Stage, The Bid for Power Stage, The Constructive Stage, and The Esprit Stage. These stages are described below:

The Polite Stage

In this stage, people become acquainted and experience first impressions. Often, at the first meeting of a group, most members tend to feel inadequate and try to hide their feelings of inadequacy. There is a high priority on wanting to be liked. People are cautious about revealing themselves and talk tends to be superficial chatter. There usually is great dependency on the group leader. There is an anxiety which diminishes as people come to know one another better. As people interact, they slowly drop their guards and per-sons are gradually seen as unique individuals with differences as well as similarities.

The Why We're Here Stage

In this stage, the group is trying to define its goals and purposes. Those who gather to form a small Christian community or group certainly know in some general sense that the group will focus on gospel values. They may be quite unsure as to what this might concretely mean. Even if the leader has a clearer understanding of the reason for the group, each group member will have to go through some process of internalizing the definition and purpose of the group. Consciously or unconsciously, each member will be focusing on questions including: "Who are these people?" "Do I belong here?" "How will this group meet my personal needs?" "Why do they need me; what do I have to contribute?" "Do I agree with the basic purpose of this group?" There may be hidden agendas—that is, individual plans to use the group for one's own purposes. These may be unconscious plans. Cliques may begin to develop. Group identity is still low. The nature and importance of the group are still vague and expectations are still uncertain. Time is needed for the group to clarify, discuss, and internalize the purpose, ground rules, and boundaries of the group.

The Bid for Power Stage

There is sometimes a reluctance to recognize the existence of power dynamics and conflict within Christian communities. However, since these are normal developments within all groups, it is unrealistic to think that such dynamics will be avoided in small Christian communities. Power dynamics and conflict are not only not bad, they are necessary if a group is to mature.

In this stage, individuals may, consciously or unconsciously, question, "How much can I influence this group?" "How much will the group and its individual members influence me?" "How much do I want to be influenced?" "Who's really important in this group?" People are concerned that they are not wasting their time and energy and that they will have some control over what happens within the group. Different individuals may surface different and, seemingly contradictory, needs and values. In a small Christian community the group and individuals can often address these questions within a common vision of community that comes from the shared reflection on scripture and the shared prayer that are a regular part of the life of the community.

It is important that, in some way, unresolved conflict issues are surfaced and dealt with directly or they will continue to smolder below the surface and the group will not be able to move with surety to the next stage.

The Constructive Stage

In this stage, there is a greater possibility for attitudinal changes. Group members really listen to one another and are open to different opinions and ideas. They share at a deeper level, trusting in the acceptance of the group. Creative thinking is encouraged and critiqued in a spirit of "give and take." There is less reluctance to challenge one another. Capitalizing on the various strengths and skills of its members, the group arrives at accurate conclusions and creative decisions. Decisions are implemented by everyone since the whole group has "ownership," that is, each person feels that his or her opinion has been heard and respected. Since there is a sense of group identity, it can be difficult to introduce new members into the group at this point. Just as the group had to progress through the three earlier stages in order to arrive at the Constructive stage, so a new member will have to experience the same process before arriving at this point of cohesiveness.

The Esprit Stage

At this point, the group experiences a high spirit of unity and group morale. There is intense group loyalty and great pleasure in being together. Emotional ties are strong and there is a high level of trust. Members look forward to sharing joys and sorrows with one another and can depend on the group for support, affirmation, and affection.

Members could begin to experience a reluctance to disturb the harmony of the group and could "backslide" to former stages as they begin to avoid conflict and any dynamic that resembles confrontation. Nurturing one another and the group could become a preoccupation. Furthermore, since the group identity is so strong and the sense of unity so intense, the introduction of new members can be disturbing for everyone unless the group consciously accepts the adjustments that will be necessary for a new person to be integrated into the group.

Adapted from
The Leadership Book
by Charles J. Keating
Paulist Press, Mahwah, NJ

REFLECTION SHEET #26

What the Leader Should Do at Each Stage

The Polite Stage:

The Why We're Here Stage:

The Bid for Power Stage:

The Constructive Stage:

The Esprit Stage:

COMMUNICATION IN THE SMALL GROUP

SAMPLE SCHEDULE

Welcome/Presentation of Aim/	
Opening Prayer	5 min.
Presentation	20 min.
Group Experience, Part 1	45 min.
Break	5 min.
Group Experience, Part 2	20 min.
Building Understanding	5 min.
Scripture Sharing/Closing Prayer	20 min.

PREPARATION

The Bible should be in a prominent position and opened to the reading from the gospel of Mark which will be read during the Scripture Sharing/ Closing Prayer segment.

If possible, you should have newsprint and markers or a blackboard and chalk to enhance the presentation of the Johari Window in the Presentation segment.

AIM

To provide an opportunity—through presentation of information, group experience, discussion, and reflection—for participants to do the following:

- grow in their understanding of the nature of communication between people;
- increase their awareness and understanding of some obstacles to effective communication;
- practice the skills of speaking clearly and concisely, listening carefully, and recapitulating others' statements accurately.

WELCOME/PRESENTATION OF AIM/OPENING PRAYER
(5 min.)

Though it's a bit of a departure from the usual format, you will be handling the Welcome, Presentation of Aim, and Opening Prayer under one umbrella and thus in a more unified fashion. It will give you an opportunity to expand your own communication skills.

> *Leader:* In this session, we will be dealing with communication. Let us begin by pausing and remembering that our God is in constant communication with us by the very fact that God loves us into existence. Let us quietly think of God communicating life to us at this very moment.
>
> (pause)

Leader: Let us quietly thank God for this gift of life.

(pause)

Leader: Let us respond by together reverently saying Amen.

All: Amen.

PRESENTATION OUTLINE

I.   Effective communication, so necessary in small groups, is facilitated by an understanding of the nature and skills of communication and a willingness to practice those skills.

    A.   The "Johari Window," a model sometimes used in describing communication in small groups, is divided into four quadrants.

        1.   In Quadrant 1, the actions, feelings, and motives are known to the person and to others.

        2.   In Quadrant 2, the actions, feelings, and motives are known by others, but not by the person, him/herself.

        3.   In Quadrant 3, the behavior, feelings, and motives are known to the individual, but not revealed to others.

        4.   In Quadrant 4, the behavior, feelings, and motives are known neither to the individual nor to others.

    B.   Obstacles to good communication include the following:

        1.   false assumptions and expectations

        2.   anxiety and needs

        3.   defensiveness

        4.   language

PRESENTATION (20 min.)

(To enhance the presentation of the Johari Window, you may opt to use a large illustration of the "Window" that could be drawn either on newsprint or a blackboard. The use of the overhead transparency for the "Window" would also be highly effective.

Ask the participants to refer to Reflection Sheet #27 on page 27 of their Workbooks and encourage them to make notes during this Presentation segment.)

The "Johari Window"

Effective communication is necessary in the development of small Christian communities. Such communication can be achieved more easily if there is some awareness of the nature of communication and some effort to practice the skills related to it.

The "Johari Window" is a model frequently used to help in the understanding of communication in groups. This model was developed by Joe Luft and Harry Ingram; the name "Johari" comes from their first names.

As you will see on Reflection Sheet #27, the "Johari Window" is divided into four quadrants. The four quadrants represent the person in relation to other persons. The basis for the divisions is an awareness of behavior, feelings, and motivations. An action, feeling, or motive belongs in a particular quadrant depending on who knows about it.

In Quadrant 1, the actions, feelings, and motives are known to the person and to others. Quadrant 1 deals with the public self—that self known by the individual and which the individual presents to others. It is the part of the window "open" to the world. When a small community first forms, ideally much communication would fall into this quadrant.

Quadrant 2 includes actions, feelings, and motives of the person which are known by others, but not by the person him/herself. It is called the "blind" quadrant—an area known to others, but not to the individ-

ual. As a small community develops, members will begin to notice both positive and negative aspects in one another. These may include undesirable traits such as the tendency to dominate or manipulate the group. Or the traits may be positive, for example, the ability to affirm another by really listening to him or her. Sometimes, those possessing these traits may be unaware of them though such traits might be quite evident to the group.

Quadrant 3 is the "hidden" quadrant. Within this quadrant are the behavior, feelings, and motivations known to the individual but not revealed to others. People very rarely share everything they are aware of in themselves with the group. While sharing will increase as trust and acceptance levels grow, it is not necessarily desirable that a person reveal everything about him/herself with the group.

Quadrant 4, the "unknown" quadrant, refers to actions, feelings, and motivations known to neither the individual nor to others. This quadrant has to do with unconscious activity of which the person and the group are not aware. Often through the experience of a small community people will grow in their awareness of themselves and of one another and will discover aspects of themselves and of others that will be surprising.

To summarize the above—when a group first comes together, for most members, Quadrant 1 is very small. People are guarded and cautious about how much they reveal of themselves. They may put on masks or play a role. As the trust level grows, individuals are able to share information from Quadrant 3. As Quadrant 1 increases in size and Quadrant 3 decreases, the person is freer and there is a greater possibility for more honest and meaningful communication.

Eventually, if the group is open and caring, individuals will receive feedback from others in the group. As this happens, information that was confined to Quadrant 2, the "blind" quadrant, moves into Quadrant 1 and the scope of communication further increases. As the group grows in sensitivity, honesty, and awareness, it is even possible that some of Quadrant 4, the "unknown" quadrant, will become apparent to the individual and the group, thus further enlarging Quadrant 1.

Misunderstanding and limited communication often occur when Quadrant 1 is very small and individuals in the group are not in touch with true behavior, feelings, and motivations. Persons will increase their "open" quadrant at different paces. However, as true community develops, communication will be marked by the increased spontaneity, decreased anxiety, greater individual self-knowledge, and more profound sharing typical of a group of people who have risked greater openness and honesty with each another. We will return to the "Johari Window" at a later session. But at this point, it is helpful to know the general theory.

OBSTACLES TO GOOD COMMUNICATION

O FALSE ASSUMPTIONS & EXPECTATIONS
• WHETHER A MESSAGE IS HEARD / ACCEPTED — OBJECTIVE JUDGMENT / SUBJECTIVE JUDGMENT

O ANXIETY AND NEEDS
• ANXIETY HINDERS RECEPTIVITY

O DEFENSIVENESS
• NOT EXPRESSING WHAT ONE REALLY THINKS OR FEELS
• SILENCE CAN BE A DEFENSIVE POSTURE
• PEOPLE SOMETIMES REACT DEFENSIVELY TO DEFENSIVENESS
• DEFENSIVE REACTION TO CONTROL OR MANIPULATION

O LANGUAGE
• WORDS, PHRASES CAN HAVE DIFFERENT MEANINGS
• VOICE, TONE, STRONG EMOTION CAN INFLUENCE COMMUNICATION

Some Obstacles to Communications

Effective communication is more difficult than most people realize. Most people have experienced a situation in which they thought they were communicat-

ing clearly with another individual or with a group, only to discover that they were considerably misunderstood. The following will explain some of these misunderstandings which become obstacles to effective communication.

False Assumptions and Expectations

Often people assume that their statements are heard, accepted, and judged objectively, when, in reality, many subjective factors are determining how their words are being received. Attitudes and values attributable to past experiences and influences affect the hearer's objectivity.

For example, a person whose background (family, work, etc.) has stressed self-control, endurance, and a rather stoical approach to life might initially judge another person's sharing of ordinary difficulties as the complaining of a somewhat weak individual. In contrast, someone who has had a long exposure to a sympathetic and nurturing environment will enter into another's even seemingly trivial problems and identify with the frustration and pain. A wide range of values and attitudes, attributable to past experience, affect both the message conveyed and how that message is received.

Anxiety and Needs

Persons in groups are influenced by their own needs for being in the group and the goals they hope such an experience will achieve. Especially in the beginning, members experience anxiety about acceptance and uncertainty about their own willingness to be part of the group. They are usually unsure about the purpose and composition of the group. Most people do their speaking and hearing at least somewhat motivated by this tentativeness and by their need to be accepted and liked. Such needs and uncertainty affect objectivity in communication.

Defensiveness

When people do not express what they really think or feel, others in the group tend to sense it. The group is also very aware of silence and reticence in some members. Members tend to read a negative rather than positive connotation into the lack of expression of thoughts and feelings and often, as a result, react defensively.

Defensiveness can also develop when individuals feel they are being controlled or manipulated by another or others in the group who have already determined the purpose and style of the group without revealing these decisions to the other members. This can happen easily in a small community if members feel that the group is being used for someone's agenda without the agreement of the group. For example, an individual member may be envisioning the group members as advocates for a particular issue and may try to steer the group in that direction without ever sufficiently discussing this pursuit with the group. Such behavior can lead to defensiveness and resentment.

Language

Language itself can be a block in communication. People assume that others assign the same meaning to words and phrases when, in reality, different definitions and understandings may co-exist in the group. For example, persons may be discussing the importance of "shared leadership" in the group. A check of individual definitions of the term "shared leadership"

may well reveal significant differences in the understanding of that phrase and concept. Voice, tone, and inflection can also confuse the listener who is trying to hear accurately. For example, someone may say, "We have great shared leadership in our parish." The words make one statement; the inflection in the word "great" could convey the opposite meaning.

Sometimes there is a confused or mixed message because there is such a strong emotional tone attached to the words; thus it is difficult to know what is really being conveyed.

The above obstacles to communication indicate the need to be sensitive to the effectiveness of communication within the group. Sensitive group leaders can be especially important in encouraging the members to strive for clarity and honesty. They can concentrate on creating a comfortable, hospitable, and affirming climate. They can invite the timid and quiet members to participate. This may be done more effectively in private. They can be alert for discrepancies in meanings and understandings and point these out to the group. They can urge group members to develop a greater sensitivity to the dynamics of good communication. They can draw on talents and skills of members in the group to help sharpen the awareness of these dynamics.

GROUP EXPERIENCE, Part 1 (45 min.)

Divide participants into sets of three people. Individuals in each group are labeled A, B, and C.

Leader: This Group Experience centers on communication.

For 5 minutes A and B will have a discussion on the following topic: Homeless people should be forcibly taken to shelters in the winter, even if they insist that they do not want to go to a shelter.

In the discussion, A will take the pro position; B will take the con position. A will make the first statement. Before B can express an idea or opinion of his or her own, B must recapitulate what A has said to A's satisfaction. A will simply nod if satisfied.

If the feedback is not satisfactory to A, B must try again until A is sure that B has captured A's idea. B may then express his or her opinion.

Before A can offer a rebuttal, A must give back the core of B's idea to B's satisfaction—and so on. Remember that this exchange will occur for about 5 minutes.

C will serve as a moderator, making sure that both A and B are listening and recapitulating before injecting their ideas into the conversation.

Let's first take about 5 minutes to think about the issue: Homeless people should be forcibly taken to shelters in the winter, even if they insist that they do not want to go to a shelter.

(Allow 5 minutes or so for thought. Then allow 5 minutes for the exchange between A and B. At the end of this 5 minutes, ask B and C to discuss the issue in the same manner, with A serving as the moderator. Allow 5 minutes for the exchange between B and C. During the discussions you may circulate to make sure that participants understand the process and are observing the ground rules.)

Leader: Now I'm adding another dimension. We're going to continue the process to discuss the same issue, but there will be a time limit. A will once again make a statement to B. This time, B must reflect A's statement to A's satisfaction *and* state his or her own idea in no more than 30 seconds. If B cannot do that, he or she forfeits the chance to state his or her idea. The goal is to sharpen listening and recapitulating skills and, at the same time, to reduce B's input only to what is essential. C will once again be the moderator.

(You will act as the timekeeper, telling the groups when 30 seconds have passed. Allow 5 minutes for the exchange between A and B. At the end of the 5 minutes, ask B and C to discuss the issue in the same manner, with A serving as the moderator. Allow 5 minutes for the exchange between B and C.)

Leader: Now we will discuss a new topic without the time limitation. A, B, and C can all participate in this discussion. They must, however, still reflect what the prior speaker has said and recapitulate to the speaker's satisfaction.

The new restriction is that all the participants must keep their eyes closed during this discussion. The goal is to become more aware of dependency on the many nonverbal clues that we give in the process of normal conversation.

Now please close your eyes and listen to the topic for discussion: Boycotting a company's product is a good and effective way of influencing that company's decisions. Begin by quietly reflecting on this topic for a few moments.

(Pause for a few moments and then ask that the discussion begin with a statement from A, B, or C. Have the participants continue the discussion for 10 minutes.

Adapted from
Groups: Theory and Experience
by Rodney W. Napier & Matti K. Gershenfeld
Houghton Mifflin Co. , 1981

BREAK (5 min.)

GROUP EXPERIENCE, Part 2 (20 min.)

Ask participants to gather in their customary small
groups and discuss the following questions.

Questions for Discussion

At what point in the exercise did you feel least comfortable? Why
were you uncomfortable?

Was the exercise annoying to you at any time? Why?

How did the time restriction affect you? Was it helpful?

What did you learn about yourself and communication when your
eyes were closed?

What did you learn about yourself in this exercise? What did you
learn about others in your group?

BUILDING UNDERSTANDING (5 min.)

Ask the participants to recall a time when they found
that effective communication was lacking in their
own small group experience. Have them write down
something that they have learned during this session
that could have helped to avoid the obstacle to
effective communication in that experience.

SCRIPTURE SHARING/CLOSING PRAYER (20 min.)

Ask for a volunteer to prepare the reading.

Leader: In this session we have been examining the nature of communication. In the gospels, we hear of many instances when the communication between Jesus and others was ineffective because people were not able to hear Jesus' message and thus misunderstood him and the nature of his reign. Let us listen to such an episode.

Reading (Mark 10:35-40)

Questions for Discussion

What do you think prevented James and John from accurately hearing what Jesus and his reign were about?

What do you think might prevent you from hearing the message of Jesus accurately?

When the discussion ends, conclude the session as follows:

Leader: Let us end by quietly, in the depth of our hearts, asking for the particular help we need to accurately hear God's voice in our lives.

The Johari Window

	KNOWN TO SELF	NOT KNOWN TO SELF
KNOWN TO OTHERS	1. OPEN	2. BLIND
NOT KNOWN TO OTHERS	3. HIDDEN	4. UNKNOWN

BUILDING COMMUNITY THROUGH LISTENING

SAMPLE SCHEDULE

Welcome/Presentation of Aim	5 min.
Opening Prayer	5 min.
Presentation	20 min.
Group Experience	45 min.
Break	5 min.
Reflection	5 min.
Scripture Sharing	15 min.
Building Understanding	5 min.
Closing Prayer	15 min.

PREPARATION

The Bible should be positioned prominently and opened to the reading from the gospel of Mark which will be read during the Scripture Sharing segment.

If possible, you should have newsprint and markers, a blackboard and chalk, or an overhead acetate and an overhead projector with the directions for the Group Experience on page 42 of this Leader's Manual already preprinted.

AIM

To provide an opportunity—through group experience, discussion, presentation of information, prayer, and reflection—for participants to do the following:

- increase their appreciation of the importance and power of effective listening;
- grow in an awareness of how to evaluate their listening;
- understand ways in which they can improve their listening skills;
- practice listening skills.

WELCOME/PRESENTATION OF AIM (5 min.)

OPENING PRAYER (5 min.)

Leader: In the name of our God who shares divinity with us,
In the name of our God who shares humanity with us,
In the name of our God who unsettles and inspires us,
Let us give praise and thanks.
In the presence of a God whose word has called the stars into being,

All: We stand in awe.

Leader: In the presence of a God whose arms have held children, whose eyes have sparkled with joy, whose ears have heard our cries and our laughter,

All: We stand in trust.

Leader: In the presence of a God whose breath has stirred within us and caused our hearts to thirst for love,

All: We stand in need.

Leader: Before you, Giver of Life, we come in faith, in search of love and truth and wholeness.

All: Be with us; hear us, we pray.

> From *More Than Words: Prayer and Ritual for Inclusive Communities*
> by Janet Schaffran & Pat Kozak
> Meyer-Stone Books, Oak Park, IL, 1988 (p. 39)

Petitions

Leader: I invite anyone who would like to share a petition to do so. We'll all respond by saying, Lord, hear our prayer.

(You may want to begin the petitions.)

Leader: Let us pray the Our Father together.

All: Our Father...

PRESENTATION OUTLINE

I.   Effective listening contributes to the development of community.
   A.   People who truly listen to each other are drawn together in a special bond of trust, openness, and understanding.
   B.   The speaker grows through good listening.
      1.   Effective listening conveys acceptance, caring, and respect.
      2.   The person who is listened to grows in a sense of self-worth.
      3.   Good listening encourages sincerity and honesty which can lead to greater self-understanding.
   C.   The listener grows through effective listening.
      1.   The listener feels valued and appreciated.
      2.   The listener broadens perceptions and outlooks.

II. Effective listening helps individuals and groups to grow spiritually.
   A.   The following are four qualities of a good listener.
      1.   vulnerability
      2.   acceptance
      3.   expectancy
      4.   constancy
   B.   Effective listening is a discipline and a sign of the healing and enlivening presence of the Spirit.

III. Effective listening is following what another is thinking and feeling, and understanding the meaning of what another is saying from that person's perspective.
   A.   Barriers to effective listening include:
      1.   the listener talking too much
      2.   the listener not listening long enough before starting to talk
      3.   the listener remaining silent and unresponsive
   B.   What follows are helps toward effective listening.
      1.   Give the speaker time.
      2.   Work at concentration.
      3.   Listen for content and feeling.
      4.   Show interest.
      5.   Ask clarifying questions.
      6.   Delay judging.

PRESENTATION (20 min.)

In Session 27, we discussed communication as speaking and listening. In this session, we will focus more specifically on the skill of effective listening. Developing relationships and building community require that people really listen to one another. Listening helps both the speaker and the hearer to grow as persons. Good listening within a group increases the trust, openness, and understanding that make for authentic community. People who truly listen to one another are drawn together in a special bond.

Effective listening conveys acceptance, caring, and respect. The person who is listened to grows in a sense of self-worth. Good listening encourages sincerity and honesty which can often enable the speaker to come to a greater self-understanding.

At the same time, the listener feels valued and appreciated. Good listening requires that the listener enter into the thinking and experience of another person and thus helps the listener to broaden perceptions and outlooks.

Good listening helps an individual and a group to grow spiritually. In his book, *On Listening to Another,*

Douglas Steere lists four qualities of a good listener. These four qualities are:

Vulnerability—Good listeners are exposed to the discomfort of having preconceived ideas changed. They run the risk of sometimes being hurt by the honesty that good listening can evoke. They become more exposed to the pain, frustration, and complexity of the human condition. In a word, they experience human limitations and yet remain hopeful because they believe that Jesus Christ has shared in their humanity.

Acceptance—Good listeners take the speaker at face value. Really listening means that the listener cannot expect the speaker to fit into his or her expectations. The speaker is respected and valued for who he or she really is. Such caring and respect for another is similar to the love that God has for each person.

Expectancy—Good listeners hope that in communicating, both speaker and listener will arrive at greater truth and greater awareness of the beauty in both speaker and hearer. There is a sense that through the honest speaking and listening both speaker and listener will be renewed. Such hope and expectancy are basic to Christian faith.

Constancy—Good listeners will patiently persevere in listening even when it is difficult, taxing, and complicated. There is a certain faithfulness to the speaker which says, "I'm with you through the 'thick and thin' of this conversation." Such a fidelity is a reflection of God's faithfulness.

For the person of faith, good listening is a discipline, but also a sign of the healing and enlivening presence of God's Spirit.

The "How To's" of Effective Listening

Effective listening is following what another is thinking and feeling. It is understanding the meaning of what another is saying from that person's perspective. The ability to listen well rarely comes naturally. It is a skill which must be learned. However, the formal and informal education of most people has emphasized the ability to speak well with very little attention paid to the ability to listen well. If small Christian communities are to realize the fullness of their potential, it is important that their members consistently work to develop their skills, not only in speaking honestly and clearly, but also in listening effectively.

Barriers to effective listening include the listener talking too much, not listening long enough before starting to talk, or, the opposite, that is, remaining silent and unresponsive for too long a period and giving little or no indication that the speaker is being heard.

ROADBLOCKS TO GOOD LISTENING

DETOUR

○ LISTENER TALKS TOO MUCH
○ STARTS TALKING BEFORE LISTENING SUFFICIENTLY
○ REMAINS SILENT AND UNRESPONSIVE FOR TOO LONG
○ GIVES NO INDICATION THAT THE SPEAKER IS HEARD

Let's consider some suggestions for developing the skill of listening as described in Reflection Sheet #28 on pages 36-37 of the Workbook.

Give people time. Do not interrupt people until they have had the opportunity to express a full thought. People speak at different paces. Adjust to their rhythm. Resist the temptation to finish their sentences for them.

Work at concentration. Don't try to remember everything the speaker is saying. Rather, grab hold of "bite-size" pieces that capture the main ideas and feelings of the speaker. Try to put yourself in the speaker's place in order to understand his or her frame of reference or point of view.

Listen for content and feeling. Listen not just to the words but to the whole person. Pay attention to facial expressions, gestures, position of the body, and tone and intensity of the voice.

Show your interest. Have eye contact with the speaker. Avoid distracting movements and gestures that may suggest a lack of interest, for example, fidgeting, crossing your arms, sneaking glances at your watch or a clock. A relaxed manner will encourage the speaker.

Ask clarifying questions. Ask questions that help you and the speaker arrive at a greater understanding. Such questions might be: "Can you tell me more about that?" "This is what I hear you saying.... Do I have it straight?" "What was that like for you?"

Delay judging. Don't make judgments too soon. Wait to hear the whole message. Premature judging can cut off the speaker's sharing before the whole picture emerges and thus diminish understanding.

***

Effective listening requires great concentration and sensitivity. Willingness to expend the effort needed for this skill will depend on whether the hearer sees a reason for listening. The listener will be influenced by whether he or she thinks the message is important to hear. Very often, listening is also related to whether the hearer respects the speaker. Often, to listen well, a person must genuinely believe that the one speaking is worthwhile and has something valuable to say.

GROUP EXPERIENCE (45 min.)

Have participants form groups of three people. One person will be Speaker 1, another Speaker 2, and the third, Speaker 3. Display the following directions.

Listen for:
- content
- feelings
- what is inferred or implied

Leader: In this Group Experience, we will be practicing our listening skills.

Speaker 1 will have 3 minutes to give a description to Speakers 2 and 3 on the following topic: One of the Most Powerful Experiences of My Life.

Speakers 2 and 3 will then have 4 minutes to recapitulate what they heard Speaker 1 say. Include content and feeling. Also tell Speaker 1 what was implied or inferred in the statement, that is, what they could assume because of what was said. Check with Speaker 1 to find out if Speaker 1 thinks they heard accurately.

After Speakers 2 and 3 have commented on Speaker 1's statement, Speaker 2 will describe an experience and the process will be repeated.

Speaker 3 will then have the opportunity to speak, and the process will be repeated a third time. Remember that it is important to comment on content, feeling, and what was inferred as well as what was actually said. I will let you know when the 3- and 4-minute periods are finished. Take 5 or so minutes now to think about the experience you will describe.

(Pause for a few minutes.)

Now, please begin with Speaker 1's statement.

(You will act as timekeeper and may also circulate to see if groups are observing the ground rules.)

When the entire process is completed, ask the participants to take 5 or so minutes to reflect on the following question.

Adapted from
A Handbook of Structured Experiences for Human Relations Training, Vol. 1
ed. by J. William Pfeiffer and John E. Jones
University Associates Publishers and Consultants, La Jolla, CA, 1974

Question for Discussion

Did you find listening on the three levels of content, feelings, and inferences easy or difficult? Explain.

(a few minutes for reflection)

After the reflection period, ask the participants to take 10 or so minutes to discuss their answers within their groups of three.

BREAK (5 min.)

REFLECTION (5 min.)

Leader: As you read the following questions, think back on how you listened to people in the conversations you had during the break. Consider the Group Experience in which you practiced listening skills. Reflect on your listening habits in general. For a few minutes, quietly reflect on the following questions and evaluate your listening skills. Which questions can you answer positively? Which questions suggest areas for improvement?

Questions To Help You Evaluate Your Listening

Do you put what you are doing out of sight and out of mind while you are listening?

Do you think about what is being said and try to understand what it means?

Do you try to understand the "why" behind what is being said?

Do you listen regardless of the person's manner of speaking or choice of words?

Do you let others finish what they are trying to say, and if they hesitate, do you encourage them to go on?

Do you sometimes restate what was said and ask if you have interpreted it correctly?

Do you withhold judgment until the person has finished?

Do you really want to hear what others are saying, or is there something going on within you that prevents you from hearing?

From *Inside Christian Community*
by Rosine Hammett, C.S.C. & Loughlan Sofield, S.T.
LeJacq Publishing, Inc., 1987 (p. 100)

SCRIPTURE SHARING (15 min.)

Ask for a volunteer to read the following passage aloud.

Reading (Mark 7:31-37)

Question for Discussion

Hearing is a gift which we often do not sufficiently value until it is diminished. Listening well helps us to grow in our appreciation of the gift of hearing. The deaf man, cured by Jesus, must have been acutely aware of each sound he heard and must have praised God for this new gift. No one had to tell him to listen well. What are some sounds that you have heard that have made you especially grateful for the gift of hearing?

BUILDING UNDERSTANDING (5 min.)

Ask the participants to reflect on the suggestions for developing better listening skills discussed during this session and to consider which suggestion they find most difficult to follow in their own listening experiences and why.

CLOSING PRAYER (15 min.)

Ask for two volunteers to prepare the readings. You can judge the length of the pauses by doing those parts of the exercise along with the participants.

Leader: We have been concentrating on listening. Our Closing Prayer is a reminder that God speaks to us through all kinds of sounds, even those that we often think of as distractions. To help us find God in all sounds, we will use an exercise from *Sadhana, A Way to God* by Anthony de Mello, a Jesuit, now deceased, whose work is known throughout the world. We'll begin by listening to a two-part reading from *Sadhana, A Way to God.*

Reader 1: In prayer, people sometimes complain about the sounds around them. The traffic in the street. The blare of a radio. A door banging. A telephone bell ringing. All of these sounds seem to intrude upon their quiet and peacefulness and to distract them.

Some sounds are considered to foster silence and prayer. Listen to the sound of a church bell toward dusk, for instance, or the sound of the birds in the early morning, or the sound of an organ playing softly in a vast church. No complaint there! Yet there is no sound, except a sound that is so loud as to cause damage to your eardrums, that need disturb your silence and peacefulness. If you learn to take all the sounds that surround you into your contemplation, you will discover that there is a deep silence in the heart of all sounds.

Reader 2: Sounds are distracting when you attempt to run away from them, when you attempt to push them out of your consciousness, when you protest that they have no right to be there. In this last instance they are both distracting and irritating. If you just accept them and become aware of them you will find them not a source of distraction and irritation but a means for attaining silence.

Leader: We are now going to do an exercise that should relax you and help you find God in the sounds around you. So, let's begin. Close your eyes. Now block your ears, take 10 deep breaths while listening to your breathing, and then place your hands in your lap while keeping your eyes closed.

(pause)

Leader (speaking softly and slowly): Now, listen attentively to all the sounds around you, to as many of them as possible...the big sounds, the small ones; the ones that are near, the ones that are distant...

(lengthy pause)

Leader: Turn even to the smallest sounds. One sound is frequently composed of many other sounds...it has variations in pitch and intensity. See how many of these nuances you can pick up.

(pause)

Leader: Now become aware, not so much of the sounds around you, as of your act of hearing.... What do you feel when you realize that you have the faculty of hearing? Gratitude...praise... joy...love...?

(pause)

Leader: Now reflect on the fact that each sound is produced and sustained by God's almighty power...God sounding all around you.... Rest in this world of sounds.... Rest in God.

(pause)

Leader: Let us conclude this prayer by saying together simple words of thanksgiving.

All: We thank you, our God, Creator of all life.

Adapted from
Sadhana, A Way to God
by Anthony de Mello
Image Books (Doubleday & Co.)
Garden City, NY, 1984 (pp. 47-49)

REFLECTION SHEET #28

Suggestions for Developing the Skill of Listening

Give people time. Do not interrupt people until they have had the opportunity to express a full thought. People speak at different paces. Adjust to their rhythm. Resist the temptation to finish their sentences for them.

Work at concentration. Don't try to remember everything the speaker is saying. Rather, grab hold of "bite-size" pieces that capture the main ideas and feelings of the speaker. Try to put yourself in the speaker's place in order to understand his or her frame of reference or point of view.

Listen for content and feeling. Listen not just to the words but to the whole person. Pay attention to facial expressions, gestures, position of the body, and tone and intensity of the voice.

Show your interest. Have eye contact with the speaker. Avoid distracting movements and gestures that may suggest a lack of interest, for example, fidgeting, crossing your arms, sneaking glances at your watch or a clock. A relaxed manner will encourage the speaker.

Ask clarifying questions. Ask questions that help you and the speaker arrive at a greater understanding. Such questions might be: "Can you tell me more about that?" "This is what I hear you saying. . . . Do I have it straight?" "What was that like for you?"

Delay judging. Don't make judgments too soon. Wait to hear the whole message. Premature judging can cut off the speaker's sharing before the whole picture emerges and thus diminish understanding.

***

Effective listening requires great concentration and sensitivity. Willingness to expend the effort needed for this skill will depend on whether the hearer sees a reason for listening. The listener will be influenced by whether he or she thinks the message is important to hear. Very often, listening is also related to whether the hearer respects the speaker. Often, to listen well, a person must genuinely believe that the one speaking is worthwhile and has something valuable to say.

FEEDBACK AND GROWTH IN THE COMMUNITY

SAMPLE SCHEDULE

Welcome/Presentation of Aim	5 min.
Opening Prayer	10 min.
Presentation, Part 1	5 min.
Group Experience, Part 1	30 min.
Break	5 min.
Presentation, Part 2	15 min.
Group Experience, Part 2	30 min.
Building Understanding	5 min.
Closing Prayer	15 min.

PREPARATION

The Bible should be in a prominent position and opened to the reading from the letter to the Eph-esians which will be read during the Opening Prayer. Ask for a volunteer to prepare this reading.

AIM

To provide an opportunity—through group experience, presentation of information, discussion, prayer, and reflection—for participants to do the following:

- increase their understanding of how relationships and community can help them to grow in self-knowledge;
- grow in awareness of the importance of feedback in relationships and community;
- learn some important points in giving good feedback;
- practice giving feedback.

WELCOME/PRESENTATION OF AIM (5 min.)

OPENING PRAYER (10 min.)

Call To Remember God's Spirit

Leader: Let us take a moment to be quiet and to remember the presence of God's Spirit within us and within this group.

(pause)

Leader: Spirit of God, let us hear your Word, that we may be formed into one body, the body of Jesus.

Reading (Ephesians 4:1-6)

Prayers for Unity

Leader: Let us pray for deeper unity within the groups and situations which mark our personal lives. I invite you to mention in prayer such a group or situation in your life and we will respond by saying, God, send forth your Spirit.

(You may want to begin.)

Leader: There are many groups and situations in our local and world communities in which there is a lack of the unity spoken about in the reading. I invite you to mention in prayer such a group or situation, and we will respond by saying, God, send forth your Spirit and renew the face of the earth.

Leader: Come, Holy Spirit, fill the hearts of your faithful.

All: That we may renew the face of the earth.

PRESENTATION OUTLINE, Part 1

I.   The "Johari Window" is divided into four quadrants which represent the person in relation to other persons.
   A.   In Quadrant 1, the actions, feelings, and motives are known to the person and to others.
   B.   In Quadrant 2, the actions, feelings, and motives are known to others, but not to the person him/herself.
   C.   In Quadrant 3, the actions, feelings, and motives are known to the person, but are not revealed to others.
   D.   In Quadrant 4, the actions, feelings, and motives are known to neither the person nor others.

PRESENTATION, Part 1 (5 min.)

In Session 27, the "Johari Window" was introduced. In this session, we will examine how some experiences in our life relate to the "Johari Window." You may wish to refer to Reflection Sheet #27 on page 27 of the Workbook during the following review of the meaning of the "Johari Window."

The "Johari Window" is divided into four quadrants. The four quadrants represent the person in relation to others. The basis for the divisions is an awareness of behavior, feelings, and motivations. An action, feeling, or motive belongs in a particular quadrant depending on who knows about it.

In Quadrant 1, the actions, feelings, and motives are known to the person and to others. It is "open" to the world.

In Quadrant 2, the actions, feelings, and motives are known to others, but not to the person him/herself. Thus, it is called the "blind" quadrant.

In Quadrant 3, the actions, feelings, and motives are known to the person, but not revealed to others. So, it is called the "hidden" quadrant.

In Quadrant 4, the actions, feelings, and motives are known to neither the person nor others. This quadrant has to do with the unconscious activity of which the person and the group are not aware; hence, it is called the "unknown" quadrant.

GROUP EXPERIENCE, Part 1 (30 min.)

Ask the participants to take about 10 or so minutes to answer the following questions.

Questions for Reflection

What is something that you know about yourself now that you did not know several years ago?

What experiences, people, or comments helped you know this about yourself?

What is something about yourself that you initially hid from a group of which you are or were a member, but eventually revealed?

What helped or prompted you to reveal this to the group?

After the 10 minutes have passed, explain to the participants that the Questions for Reflection prompted them to think about experiences in which, according to the Johari Window, they moved information from Quadrants 2 and 3 to Quadrant 1.

Ask them to continue this Group Experience by discussing the following questions in their small groups. You should allow about 20 minutes for this discussion.

Questions for Discussion

As you think back on the experiences you noted in your responses to the Questions for Reflection, what do you think were some positive aspects of discovering the new information about yourself? What were some positive aspects of revealing the hidden information about yourself to the group?

Were there negative aspects to either of the above experiences?

BREAK (5 min.)

PRESENTATION OUTLINE, Part 2

II. Mutuality is fundamental to the small Christian community.
   A. Mutuality implies the respect that is found among equals.
   B. Mutuality is the capacity of persons to share their perceptions, feelings, wants, needs, beliefs, and knowledge with each other and to understand and respect the differences among them.
   C. In communities of mutuality, persons grow in their ability and willingness to do the following:
      1. share themselves and their lives
      2. understand other members and their lives
      3. give positive and negative feedback
      4. receive feedback

III. In feedback, persons give their observations, feelings, and reactions to another's ideas and behavior.
   A. Feedback enables individuals to grow and bond more deeply and honestly.
   B. Feedback enables persons to know if communication is being given and received accurately.
   C. Feedback helps persons to know how they appear to the community.
   D. Feedback facilitates self-knowledge.
   E. Feedback enables persons to know if they share common perceptions.

IV. What follows are suggestions for giving feedback.
   A. Be sure there is trust, caring, acceptance, and openness before giving negative feedback.
   B. Present feedback clearly and objectively.
   C. Avoid interpreting motives or evaluating.
   D. Give feedback related to recent behavior.
   E. Be specific.

MUTUALITY
IS FUNDAMENTAL TO
SMALL CHRISTIAN COMMUNITIES

MUTUALITY
IMPLIES THE *Respect*
THAT IS FOUND AMONG EQUALS

IN COMMUNITIES OF MUTUALITY
PEOPLE:
+ SHARE THEMSELVES + THEIR LIVES
+ UNDERSTAND OTHER MEMBERS
    AND THEIR LIVES
+ GIVE POSITIVE AND NEGATIVE
    FEEDBACK
+ RECEIVE FEEDBACK WITH
    OPENNESS

The authentic small Christian community tries to be the body of Christ. At the heart of that effort is the struggle to truly respect one another, to speak freely, and to listen well. Mutuality is fundamental in a small Christian community. Mutuality implies the respect that is found among equals. In their book, *Dangerous Memories,* Bernard Lee and Michael Cowan define mutuality as "the capacity of persons to share their perceptions, feelings, wants, needs, beliefs and knowledge appropriately with each other, and to understand accurately and respect the differences that exist among them as these emerge in the community's conversation" (p. 124).

According to Lee and Cowan, if mutuality is to characterize the relationships in a community, the members must be able and willing to do the following:

A. tell the events, feelings, facts, experiences, etc., of their lives;

B. understand accurately the events, experiences, and feelings of other members' lives;

C. give constructive positive and negative feedback to other members at appropriate moments;

D. receive feedback from others with openness.

Through feedback, persons give their observations, feelings, and reactions to another's ideas and behavior. Feedback can be positive, for example, "Your facilitation really kept our meeting on track when it looked as if we were going to wander all over the place." Feedback can be negative, for example, "Ann, when you talk about this conflict with your daughter, it sounds to me like you don't really listen to what she's saying." Or, "Joe, that comment you made during the meeting sounded sarcastic to me."

IN FEEDBACK
PEOPLE GIVE THEIR
OBSERVATIONS, FEELINGS AND
REACTIONS TO OTHERS' IDEAS
AND BEHAVIOR

FEEDBACK
○ ENABLES GROWTH AND BONDING
○ HELPS DETERMINE IF COMMUNICATION
    IS ACTUALLY TAKING PLACE
○ MIRRORS COMMUNITY REACTION
    FOR A PERSON
○ FACILITATES SELF KNOWLEDGE
○ ENABLES DISCERNMENT OF
    WHETHER OR NOT MEMBERS
    SHARE COMMON PERCEPTIONS

Through feedback, especially when it takes place in a spirit of mutuality, individuals can grow and members of groups can become more deeply and honestly bonded to one another.

Through feedback, we find out whether the message intended is the message that is actually received.

Sometimes, misunderstandings occur in a group because statements are misinterpreted. A good leader will be sensitive to the possibility of such misinterpretation and will tell the speaker what his or her statement seems to be conveying. For example, "Tom, that statement you just made sounds as if you don't think we're prayerful people. Is that what you meant?"

Feedback helps us to know how we appear to the community. Through feedback, areas of ourselves to which we are blind (Quadrant 2 of the "Johari Window") are revealed to us (as they become part of Quadrant 1, the "known" quadrant). We can also learn how our ideas and behavior affect others in the community and whether we share common perceptions with other members of the group.

What follows are some suggestions for giving feedback.

- Be sure there is at least some level of trust, caring, acceptance, and openness before giving negative feedback. Be cautious about giving negative feedback in the very early stages of a group's development.

- Present feedback clearly and objectively.

- Avoid interpreting motives or evaluating. For example, "Sue, I've noticed that you're usually late, disrupting the group when you come in,"

rather than "Sue, you're always late. I think that's rude, and you're probably trying to get attention from the group."

- Give feedback related to very recent behavior; feedback which occurs after a time lapse is harder to give, hear, and receive.

- Be specific, not general, in giving feedback. For example, "Alice, you were great in organizing the volunteers and following through on our outreach project," is better than "Alice, you did a great job on our outreach project."

SUGGESTIONS FOR GIVING FEEDBACK

- BE SURE OF TRUST AND ACCEPTANCE LEVELS BEFORE GIVING NEGATIVE FEEDBACK
- BE CLEAR AND OBJECTIVE
- AVOID INTERPRETING MOTIVES
- AVOID EVALUATING
- LIMIT FEEDBACK TO RECENT EVENTS
- BE SPECIFIC

GROUP EXPERIENCE, Part 2 (30 min.)

Ask the participants to take about 5 or so minutes to
answer the following questions. Explain that the
group referred to in the Questions for Reflection is
the group each participant has worked with during
the *Called To Lead* sessions.

Questions for Reflection

Which member of the group is most similar to me?

How is this person similar to me?

Which member of the group is most dissimilar to me?

How is this person dissimilar to me?

After the 5 minutes have passed, have the participants return to their small groups if they are not cur-
rently in them. Ask each person to simply share and
not discuss the responses to the Questions for
Reflection, including the characteristics upon which
the judgments were made. Allow 5 minutes for this
sharing.

After 5 minutes have passed, explain to the participants that what they just did was a form of giving
feedback. Ask them to take the next 20 minutes or
so to discuss the following questions.

Questions for Discussion

If you were mentioned as similar or dissimilar to another member
of the group, do you agree or disagree with each reason?

Can the group give specific examples from your behavior which
support the reasons given?

BUILDING UNDERSTANDING (15 min.)

Ask the participants to consider how difficult it was
to determine which group members were similar and
dissimilar to them and why.

CLOSING PRAYER (15 min.)

Ask for a volunteer to prepare the scripture reading.

Leader: God, who forms us into one body, open our
hearts and our minds that we may know your unity.

Reading (Romans 12:4-8)

Petitions

Leader: All of us, at this period in time, at this moment
in our particular history, need certain gifts if we are to
be fully healthy members of the body of Christ. I invite
you to mention the particular gift that you need. We
will respond by saying, O God, hear our prayer.

(pause)

Thanksgiving

Leader: All of us have gifts that we have been given
for the building up of the body of Christ. I invite you
to thank God for a person in the group and for a gift
that person brings to the community by mentioning
the person's name and his or her particular gift. We
will respond by saying, We thank you, God.

(pause)

Concluding Song

Leader: Let us close by singing together, "Spirit of the
Living God."

CONFLICT—MAKING IT WORK FOR THE GROUP

SAMPLE SCHEDULE

Welcome/Presentation of Aim	5 min.
Opening Prayer	5 min.
Presentation, Part 1	5 min.
Group Experience, Part 1	15 min.
Presentation, Part 2	20 min.
Break	5 min.
Group Experience, Part 2	35 min.
Scripture Sharing	20 min.
Building Understanding	5 min.
Closing Prayer	5 min.

PREPARATION

The Bible should be in a prominent position and opened to the beginning of the reading from the Acts of the Apostles which will be read during the Scripture Sharing segment.

Designate which groups will pray the lines indicated with a " 1." and which will pray the lines indicated with a "2." during the Opening Prayer.

AIM

To provide an opportunity—through group experience, discussion, presentation of information, prayer, and reflection—for participants to grow in their awareness, understanding, and appreciation of the following:

- their understanding and appreciation of the value of conflict;
- a greater awareness of their own attitudes and behavior in conflict;
- their understanding of the nature of conflict;
- ways of managing and resolving conflict;
- the practice of conflict management skills.

WELCOME/PRESENTATION OF AIM (5 min.)

OPENING PRAYER (5 min.)

Leader: O God of life, we experience so many conflicts, both in our personal lives and in the world around us. Yet, in these conflicts, we believe that your creative, redeeming, and loving presence is with us, enabling us to grow and to become more like you. Together, we proclaim our belief in you.

1. We believe in God, who called the world into being; who created men and women and set them free to live in love, in obedience, and community.

2. We believe in God, who because of love for all creation, entered the world to share our humanity, to rejoice and to experience darkness, to set before us the paths of life and death; to be rejected, to die, but finally to conquer death through resurrection and to bind the world back to God.

1. We believe in God who invites us into the community of the church that we may, through faith and communion, experience God's uplifting and sustaining grace; that we may fulfill our human responsibilities and reach out to our neighbors, listening to them and understanding their needs; that we may work to bring healing and wholeness to a ruptured and uncertain world…and that we may rejoice in the constancy of nature and the joy of life itself.

2. We believe in God whose word teaches us that the wheat and the tares grow together; that the paths of life and death, good and evil, too often converge…choices are not clearly defined…but we confidently and responsibly tread the path we choose with guidance from our community of faith.

1. We believe in God who is present and working in this world through men and women. We sense God's purpose in a spark of light here and there as humankind struggles to keep a human face.

2. We know God's purpose as we watch children at play…hope burn anew in each generation…perhaps to be quickly extinguished, perhaps to continue to burn brightly. But for that hope we give thanks.

All: Amen.

> Adapted from
> *No Longer Strangers: A Resource for Women and Worship*
> ed. by Iben Gjerbing and Katherine Kinnamon
> WCC Publications, Geneva, 1983

PRESENTATION OUTLINE, Part 1

I. Conflict is inevitable in groups.
   A. What follows are ways in which people try to avoid conflicts:
      1. denial
      2. avoiding the persons involved
      3. making a joke out of the disagreement
      4. giving in even when there is no agreement
      5. postponing dealing with the issue
   B. Unaddressed conflict will lead to distrust, tension, and apathy.
   C. Conflict, when managed or resolved, can lead to increased unity, strength, energy, and creativity within groups.

II. The following questions are helpful in reflecting on one's attitudes toward conflict:
   A. Do I usually try to avoid conflict? If I do, what are my usual avoidance techniques?
   B. Am I aware of my needs, wants, and emotions in conflict situations?
   C. Can I usually believe that those with whom I am in conflict are basically good, or do I find myself negatively judging their motives and character?
   D. Am I able to try to identify their needs and wants?
   E. Do I become competitive so that the conflict becomes largely a win/lose situation?

PRESENTATION, Part 1 (5 min.)

Whenever two or more human beings are together for a length of time, there will be conflict. Sometimes church groups, especially groups like small Christian communities, which are so involved in reflection and discussions on gospel values, feel that conflict is contradictory to the very nature of the group. However, conflict is part of the human condition and, as such, has been part of the Christian community since its beginning, as shown in various episodes found in the gospels and in the Acts of the Apostles.

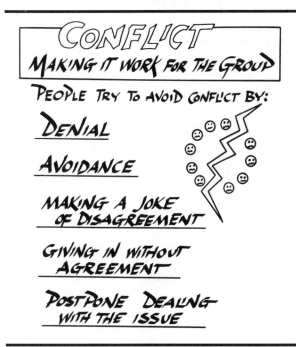

Most of us have a tendency to try to avoid conflict. Some typical avoidance techniques include denial, avoiding the persons involved, making a joke out of the disagreement, giving in even when there is no agreement, or postponing dealing with the issue.

Conflicts do not usually resolve themselves. If the conflict is over something very insignificant, it may disappear with time. Sometimes, a leader of a group can identify a problem as obviously coming from one person's self-interest and, if their relationship is positive, the leader may be able to resolve the issue by speaking to the person privately. However, most conflicts, if not addressed, will lead to ongoing distrust, tension, and apathy. Conversely, when conflict in a group is dealt with, managed, or resolved, the group often experiences an increased sense of unity, cohesion, strength, energy, and creativity. Not all conflict can be resolved. Some conflict must be managed on an ongoing basis so that persons and groups can relate with some degree of harmony.

In considering how to deal with conflict, it is helpful to reflect on one's own attitudes and history in this matter. The following questions found in section II. of the Presentation Outline on page 46 of the Workbook could help in this reflection:

- Do I usually try to avoid conflict? If I do, what are my usual avoidance techniques?

- Am I aware of my needs, wants, and emotions in conflict situations?

- Can I usually believe that those with whom I am in conflict are basically good, or do I find myself negatively judging their motives and character?

- Am I able to try to identify their needs and wants?

- Do I become competitive so that the conflict becomes largely a win/lose situation?

Honest answers to the preceding questions could help you to better understand yourself and others, and prepare you to manage and resolve conflicts more effectively.

GROUP EXPERIENCE, Part 1 (15 min.)

Ask each participant to join with one other person for this Group Experience. Have each participant privately recall a conflict in which he or she was involved.

(pause)

Ask the participants to refer to the questions on conflict management from section II. of the Presentation Outline in their Workbooks and reflect on how they would answer these questions in relation to their particular conflict situation.

After 5 or so minutes, ask each pair to discuss the following questions.

Questions for Discussion

As you reflected on the questions and this particular conflict, what did you think were your strengths in dealing with the conflict?

What were your weaknesses?

PRESENTATION OUTLINE, Part 2

III. What follows are suggestions for managing conflict more effectively:

    A. Diagnose the conflict.

        1. Conflicts often relate to values.

        2. Some conflicts relate to specific, concrete, easily defined problems.

        3. Sometimes, conflicts are fed by poor communication.

        4. Self-esteem is frequently a basic issue in conflicts.

    B. Reduce the emotional level and help persons to listen to one another.

        1. Remain calm and show compassion and caring to all involved.

        2. Remind the group of the things they share in common.

        3. Suggest that the group take time for reflection and prayer.

        4. Encourage the members to listen carefully to each other.

        5. Help communication by paraphrasing, clarifying, and summarizing.

    C. Solve the problem. Some conflicts involve specific, concrete problems that can be solved. What follows are some suggestions for solving problems:

        1. Make sure that the problem is clearly understood, and that the group knows as many of the related details as possible.

        2. Brainstorm possible solutions without discussing or evaluating proposals.

        3. Make sure that everyone understands each proposal.

        4. Cite similarities and differences in proposals.

        5. Discuss the "pros" and "cons" of each proposal, allowing for proposals to be combined with or modified by others.

        6. Decide on the best proposal or solution.

PRESENTATION, Part 2 (20 min.)

While most of us would like to see it just go away, conflict is inevitable in human relationships. If, over a period of time, no conflict emerges within a group, it is probably being repressed. Such repression will eventually sap the group of its life and leave it superficial and apathetic. On the other hand, in learning to deal with conflict a group can experience new vitality and deeper relationships.

The following suggestions for managing conflict more effectively are found in outline form in the Presentation Outline on pages 47-48 of the Workbook.

Diagnose the Conflict

Take the time to analyze the problem. Sometimes what first appears as the issue is simply a symptom of the real conflict. Conflict within the Christian community often relates to values. For example, members of a small Christian community may disagree on the amount of time and energy they want to spend on more formal learning experiences. There are value questions related to issues such as this, and it is helpful if members of the group can articulate the values underlying the issue.

Some conflicts relate to specific, concrete, and easily defined problems. For example, members of the group may disagree on the best way to present the concept of small Christian communities at a diocesan workshop they have been asked to conduct. Such issues can sometimes be resolved through the application of problem-solving skills which we will discuss later in this session.

Sometimes conflicts are fed by poor communication. A group's leader can be especially helpful in making sure that all members of the group are receiving the same information. In discussions in the group, especially when there is some tension, the leader can assist by paraphrasing statements to make sure all the members have a common understanding of what is being said.

It is important to remember that self-esteem is frequently a basic issue in conflicts. People have a need to maintain a sense of self-esteem. If they feel their self-esteem is threatened, they tend to become defensive and can feel a need to attack whoever or whatever is presenting the threat. The conflict can easily become a win/lose situation. The other person or persons are now perceived as the opposition, and any spirit of cooperation that existed is replaced by a spirit of competition. When people are competing with one another, they tend to evaluate everything on the basis of whether it is supportive of their position. They block out those things that do not support their point of view. At this point, the major objective is to win. The leader can help, in such a situation, by trying to reduce the increased emotional level often accompanying such a discussion, and by enabling persons to listen to one another.

Reduce the Emotional Level and Help Persons Listen to One Another

It is important that the leader try to remain calm and emotionally distanced in such a situation. He or she will then be in a better position to encourage a caring climate in which people can feel that they are heard and understood. A compassionate attitude toward all who are involved in the conflict can enable others to express greater caring and compassion.

The leader can remind the group of the many things they share in common. This is especially true in a small Christian community in which members have regularly acknowledged their unity in faith.

The leader can suggest that the group take some quiet time for reflection and prayer. Reflection questions can include some of the questions we worked through during the Group Experience. Such questions should help the members think about the cause of the conflict and the reasons for their strong positions and emotional involvement.

The listening skills that have been discussed in previous sessions play an important role in managing conflict. Clarifying, paraphrasing, and summarizing help in resolving confusion and ambiguity. The leader could encourage members to try to really listen to each other. Such encouragement can be especially effective if in the past the group has learned and practiced specific listening skills. Conflict is reduced when the parties involved feel that they are really being heard and that their positions are genuinely understood.

Solve the Problem

Some conflicts involve concrete problems that can be solved. For example, the conflict cited earlier, in which members of a small group may disagree on the best way to present the concept of small Christian communities in a diocesan workshop, can be resolved. A structured process can help the group reach such a resolution. This process could include the following steps:

–   Make sure that the problem is clearly understood and that the group knows as many of the related details as possible. For example, in the case of the diocesan workshop: How long is the workshop? About how many will be attending? What kinds of people will be attending? What time of the day and at what point in the schedule will the workshop be presented?

–   Brainstorm possible solutions. Have members propose as many ways of solving the problem as possible without discussion or evaluation.

–   Make sure that everyone understands each proposal.

–   Cite similarities and differences in proposals.

–   Discuss the "pros" and "cons" of each proposal. Some proposals may be combined. Some proposals may be modified to include ideas from other proposals.

–   Decide on the best proposal or solution.

BREAK (5 min.)

Explain to the participants that they will be doing some role playing to sharpen their conflict management skills. Have them divide their small group in two so that half will hold one position in the disagreement and half will hold the opposite position. Underscore that the object of this Group Experience is for the opposing segments to enter into a conflict management effort. Tell them that even if they cannot resolve the conflict in the allotted time, they should at least make an honest effort to enter into the conflict management process without sacrificing their convictions. Designate which group members will assume Role Description 1 and which will assume Role Description 2. Have both sides follow the Directions for Playing the Role. Ask the participants to take a few minutes to read the Role Description that will apply to them and really get into the role described.

Allow 20 minutes for the participants to deal with the disagreement.

Role Description 1

You are a strong believer in the church's social responsibility. You think that your small group should take a more active role in social issues. You are especially concerned that their outreach include taking some stands on justice issues. Specifically, you want the group to speak out and become involved in supporting a local proposal for the construction of low and moderate income housing. While the members generally support the town proposal, some believe the issue is too controversial for the group at this time.

Role Description 2

You believe that your small group should be involved in outreach activities. Lately, however, several members of the group have suggested that the group become more involved in controversial justice issues. They are proposing that, as an outreach project, the group support a town proposal for low and moderate income housing. You believe that, while the members generally support the town proposal, the group is not ready for this kind of involvement. You think it is too controversial and that the group should be stronger before taking it on. You feel that the group needs more formation especially in the church's social teaching, and more prayer and reflection on scripture before tackling such a difficult problem.

Directions for Playing the Role

Try to get into the thinking and feelings of the role. Be in touch with changes in your feelings as you play the role.

Use the suggestions found in the Presentation Outline on pages 47-48 of the Workbook to try to manage the conflict.

Don't be rigidly resistant; but don't accept solutions that you really can't agree with.

After 20 minutes, have participants discuss the following questions in their small groups.

Questions for Discussion

What were specific moments in the discussion when there was progress in managing the conflict or disagreement? What contributed to the progress?

What were specific moments in the discussion when it was difficult to manage the conflict or disagreement? Why was it difficult?

SCRIPTURE SHARING (20 min.)

Ask for four volunteers to prepare the following readings.

Leader: Throughout history, there have been many conflicts within the Christian community. In the following scripture passage, we will hear about one of the most important conflicts that arose in the early church. If possible, read along in your Bible, and as you read and listen to the description of this conflict, pay special attention to how the Spirit is active within the community, helping good come from this dispute.

Reading 1 (Acts 15:1-12)

Reading 2 (Acts 15:13-21)

Reading 3 (Acts 15:22-29)

Reading 4 (Acts 15:30-35)

After the readings are completed, ask the participants to discuss the following questions.

Questions for Discussion

What good came from this dispute in the early church?

What good came from a conflict in your parish or small group community?

BUILDING UNDERSTANDING (5 min.)

Ask the participants to reflect on their level of comfort during the conflict management process during the Group Experience and why it was a comfortable or uncomfortable situation for them.

CLOSING PRAYER (5 min.)

Ask for a volunteer to prepare the reading. Tell the person to pause briefly before beginning the reading.

Call to Openness

Leader: We will hear a brief reading from the gospel according to Mark. As you listen to this reading, note any word or phrase that is especially meaningful to you. Let us now quiet ourselves and open our hearts and minds to the Word of God.

(brief pause)

Reading (Mark 9:33-35)

Leader: I invite you to share just the word or phrase that was especially meaningful to you in this reading. Simply speak this word or phrase quietly.

(Allow time for participants to speak their words.)

Concluding Song

Leader: Let us close by singing together, "Let There Be Peace on Earth."

CONSENSUS—AN OPTION FOR UNITY

SAMPLE SCHEDULE

Welcome/Presentation of Aim	5 min.
Opening Prayer	5 min.
Presentation, Part 1	15 min.
Group Experience	45 min.
Break	5 min.
Presentation, Part 2	15 min.
Scripture Sharing	20 min.
Building Understanding	5 min.
Closing Prayer	5 min.

PREPARATION

The Bible should be in a prominent position and opened to the reading from the letter to the Ephesians which will be read during the Scripture Sharing segment.

Set up a record player, cassette player, or CD player with instrumental music which will continue to play softly throughout the Opening Prayer.

Designate which groups will pray the verses indicated with a " 1." and which will pray the verses indicated with a "2." during the Opening Prayer.

AIM

To provide an opportunity—through prayer, discussion, presentation of information, and scripture sharing—for participants to grow in their awareness, understanding, and appreciation of the following:

- the value of reaching a decision by consensus;
- the requirements necessary for reaching a decision through consensus;
- the skills needed for consensus decision-making.

WELCOME/PRESENTATION OF AIM (5 min.)

OPENING PRAYER (5 min.)

Call to Quiet

Leader: We come from busy lives. Let us quiet ourselves, remembering that we are in the presence of God.

(Pause for a few moments of reflection.)

Leader: Let us join together in prayer.

A Meeting

1. Today we gather.
   Meeting together to consider
   where we stand
   and who we are.

2. We come to order ourselves
   into a new sense of order according to our progress
   from the last gathering to this one.

1. Be with us, O God,
   in this space and time
   as we affirm and shape the changes
   in our understanding of the Way.

2. We desire not to fly apart
   in garish fantasy of vision
   but rather to move the boundaries
   that we have set before
   in order to encompass and embrace
   the living and breathing growth
   of each and all.

1. We work in prayer and dialogue.
   In going back to see where we have been,
   we steady ourselves
   for the journey forward today.

2. We are here
   to reconcile all that we were,
   our trust…our hopelessness
   our joy…our despair
   our confirming…our betrayal.…
   To confess, absolve, reconcile, renew.
   To be all that we can be.

1. To set firm a pathway that is possible.
   Possible for us to walk until we meet again
   to reassess the journey
   and again set firm a pathway.

2. Each step along the way we clear the stones and obstacles,
   healing and refreshing each other.
   We listen openly to each tale of travel and
   hear each one's proposal for the time ahead.

1. Knowing you are here, God,
   we are freer in our interaction,
   more daring in the sharing of our personal visions,
   loving in our confrontation,
   deeply silent in consideration and
   accepting in the choices that for a little while will help
   us to define our actions
   until broader definitions draw us on.

2. In this your presence,
   we meet to order ourselves anew,
   to consider where we stand and who we are.
   Today we gather.

Taken from *Miryam of Nazareth*
by Ann Johnson

PRESENTATION OUTLINE, Part 1

I. Consensus is an especially appropriate way for small Christian communities to come to decisions.
   A. In a consensus style of decision-making, all participants contribute to the decision-making process and all share in the final decision.
   B. Consensus places a high priority on the unity of the group, while respecting the individual.
   C. The input of all members often produces a better decision.

D. Differences of opinion are seen as enriching and not as obstacles.

E. Compromise and harmonizing are emphasized rather than competition.

II. Consensus requires effort.

A. Members must be committed to finding an answer or solution acceptable to all.

B. A level of trust must exist.

C. Good communication skills must be applied.

D. Consensus requires willingness to spend the necessary time involved.

E. There must be a willingness and ability to deal with differences and sometimes conflict.

F. A decision reached through consensus will usually be enthusiastically supported and implemented by the group.

III. What follows are important points to consider before beginning a consensus process.

A. The question should be significant enough to warrant the amount of time and energy that a consensus process will require.

B. Adequate information on the topic should be available to each member of the group.

C. Silence does not necessarily mean consent. Quiet members should be encouraged to express their thinking.
Each member of the group should indicate willingness to accept the decision.

D. Allow sufficient time for the process. Time should not be a pressure which forces the group into a premature decision.

E. View differences of opinion and conflict as helpful allies in arriving at the best decision.

F. Practice good communication skills. Listen well and speak clearly and directly.

G. Make distinctions among facts, opinions, and feelings. All three are important in considering possible decisions.

H. Avoid competitiveness.

I. Consider the size of the group. Larger groups will usually require more complex processes and often a skilled facilitator to reach consensus.

+ APPROPRIATE FOR SCCs

+ ESPECIALLY VALUABLE FOR SERIOUS DECISIONS

In Consensus

○ ALL PARTICIPANTS CONTRIBUTE TO THE PROCESS AND SHARE IN THE FINAL DECISION

○ HIGH PRIORITY PLACED ON UNITY OF THE GROUP WHILE RESPECTING THE INDIVIDUAL

○ THE INPUT OF ALL PRODUCES A BETTER DECISION

○ DIFFERENCES ARE SEEN AS ENRICHING NOT AS OBSTACLES

○ COMPROMISE/HARMONIZING EMPHASIZED RATHER THAT COMPETITION

○ CONSENSUS DECISIONS ARE USUALLY ENTHUSIASTICALLY SUPPORTED AND IMPLEMENTED

Small communities make various decisions. Some are relatively minor, for example, deciding where to meet. Other decisions are more important and have greater implications for the life of the group, for example, whether the community should be involved in a particular outreach effort. In a small Christian community, where members are striving to understand and respect one another and where each person's opinion is judged valuable, decisions are appropriately made in a spirit of consensus. In more serious decisions, a process for reaching consensus may be necessary.

Consensus is a method of decision-making in which all participants contribute to the decision-making process and all members share in the final decision. The process provides a forum in which input is required from all participants, thus emphasizing the unity of the group while respecting the individual and ultimately producing more options to reach a better decision. Differences of opinion are seen as enrich-

ing and not as obstacles. The emphasis is on compromise and harmonizing, rather than on competition. However, consensus does not mean that everyone agrees with the decision, but rather that everyone can live with it and be willing to help in its implementation. Sometimes, consensus may involve agreement to give the decision an experimental try for a determined period of time, followed by evaluation and reconsideration.

Consensus requires effort. The members of the group must be committed to finding an answer or solution that is acceptable to all. A level of trust must exist within the group so that members can be honest, open, and direct in expressing their ideas and opinions. The communication skills discussed in previous sessions are necessary for the process to work well. The group must have the time to consider opinions, alternatives, and the implications and consequences of different decisions. There must be the willingness and ability to deal with differences and possibly with conflict. The effort to achieve consensus, however, is well worth it. The group that reaches true consensus will readily and, usually, enthusiastically "own," support, and implement the decision.

○ MEMBERS MUST BE COMMITTED TO FINDING A SOLUTION ACCEPTABLE TO ALL

○ A LEVEL OF TRUST MUST EXIST

○ GOOD COMMUNICATION SKILLS MUST BE APPLIED

○ MUST HAVE WILLINGNESS TO SPEND NECESSARY TIME

○ MUST HAVE WILLINGNESS TO DEAL WITH DIFFERENCES AND SOMETIMES CONFLICT

The following important points for the group to consider and to agree to before beginning a consensus process are found in outline form in the Presentation Outline on pages 55-57 of the Workbook.

- The question should be significant enough to warrant the amount of time and energy that a consensus process will require. Simple issues are easily and effectively decided by brief discussion or, if necessary, by the raising of hands. Church groups, such as small Christian communities, will often find an issue is significant enough to use consensus because it relates to values of great importance to them, for example, the unity of the group, the importance and dignity of individuals, the relationship with the wider parish, or fidelity to the mission to which they are committed.

- Adequate information on the topic should be available to each member of the group. For the Christian community, this information might include pertinent excerpts from documents of the church and helpful reflective passages from scripture. Often, if the decision requires knowledge and understanding of much information, it is helpful for members to receive information before the consensus session or to have a prior session to become well informed.

- Silence does not necessarily mean consent. Quiet members should be encouraged to express their thinking. Each member of the group should indicate willingness to accept the decision before closure on the issue.

- Allow sufficient time for the process. Time should not be a pressure which forces the group into a premature decision.

- View differences of opinion and conflict as helpful allies in arriving at the best decision.

- Practice good communication skills. Listen well and speak clearly and directly.

- Make distinctions among facts, opinions, and feelings. All three are important in considering possible decisions. Both the listener and the hearer should feel free to point out such distinctions.

- Avoid competitiveness. Rather, see success not as the victory of an individual's idea, but rather as consensus reached by the group.

- Consider the size of the group. The consensus process presented in this session is best suited to a group of not more than twenty. As the number of persons increases, reaching consensus can become more difficult and will require a more complex process facilitated by someone skilled in such processes.

GROUP EXPERIENCE (45 min.)

Leader: Achieving consensus on a serious issue takes time and preparation. In this Group Experience, we will be concentrating on using the skills that are necessary to effectively work for consensus.

Have the participants turn to Reflection Sheet #29 on pages 63-64 of their Workbooks. Ask them to take about 5 minutes to read and follow the directions individually for the ranking of activities.

After 5 or so minutes, ask the participants to work within their small group to reach a consensus in ranking the same items. Suggest to the participants that they review the points on working toward a consensus from section III. of the Presentation Outline in their Workbooks before beginning the consensus process. Tell them that they should use Reflection Sheet #30 on pages 65-66 of their Workbooks as they take approximately 25 minutes to reach a consensus.

After 25 or so minutes, ask the participants to turn to Reflection Sheet #31 on page 67 of their Workbooks to see the actual rankings given to the items by the group of Core Catholics and then to continue with the discussion questions that follow.

Questions for Discussion

How did your individual rankings compare with the rankings of the "Core Catholics"?

How did your group's rankings compare with the rankings of the "Core Catholics"?

What specific suggestions, ideas, and behaviors helped the consensus-reaching process of the group?

What specific suggestions, ideas, and behaviors hindered the consensus-reaching process of the group?

What positive and negative feelings did you experience during the process?

(Allow approximately 15 minutes for discussion.)

BREAK (5 min.)

PRESENTATION OUTLINE, Part 2

IV. What follows is a process that can be used when trying to reach consensus on a particular issue.

    A.   Begin with a firm proposal that is clearly stated.

    B.   Make sure that all members of the group have a common understanding of consensus and are committed to a willingness to compromise and to arrive at a common conclusion.

    C.   Share all information relative to the proposal with all members of the group.

    D.   Pray for the guidance of the Holy Spirit.

    E.   Ask each member to share his or her position on the issue.

    F.   Have members give all the "cons" of the issue. List the "cons."

    G.   Quietly reflect and pray over the "cons."

    H.   Have members give all the "pros" of the issue. List the "pros."

    I.   Quietly reflect and pray over the "pros."

    J.   Open discussion. Are there clarifications, suggestions, new ideas, an integration of ideas?

    K.   Check for possible consensus. Have each person state the position he or she can live with.

    L.   If consensus is not reached at this point, re-evaluate the "pros" and "cons" lists, identify and concentrate on critical points, and try to integrate further the thinking of the group.

    M.   Continue to encourage an atmosphere of optimism and mutual support.

    N.   When the leader feels that consensus has been reached, he or she should state the consensus that he or she thinks the group has reached and check with each member as to whether he or she can live with the statement. If he or she cannot, ask him or her if there are changes he or she could offer which would make the statement acceptable to him or her. Ask if the other members of the group can accept the changes.

    O.   If consensus cannot be reached, the group may decide to table the issue, or, if necessary, decide on another way to reach a decision.

    P.   Thank God for the efforts and unity of the group in the process.

PRESENTATION, Part 2 (15 min.)

The following is a process that can be used when groups are trying to reach consensus on a specific issue. An outline of the process is found in the Presentation Outline, Part 2, on pages 58-59 of your Workbooks. We'll go through the process and apply it to a particular issue.

- Begin with a firm proposal that is clearly stated. We'll use the following proposal to illustrate the consensus process.

   Our small community has been meeting regularly for three years. We are a closely knit group that shares prayer and scripture together at a deep level. We have been involved in several outreach projects and are becoming more concerned with how our lifestyle, as individuals and within our families, reflects gospel values of simplicity, justice, and concern for the environment. Presently, there is a concentrated effort in the parish to form new small communities. Existing groups have been encouraged by the small Christian community core group to consider re-grouping so that the new groups may have the experience of members who have been in a good small community.

The steps for a consensus process might apply to this issue as follows:

- Make sure that all members of the group have a common understanding of consensus and are committed to a willingness to compromise and to arrive at a common conclusion.

Understanding and commitment of individual members and the group can be ascertained through a discussion of both the information on this process for reaching consensus and the points to consider in working toward consensus that we have already worked with.

- Share all information relative to the proposal with all members of the group.

Information relative to the above proposal might include answers to the following questions:

   Who is asking for the re-grouping and why? How many new groups may be forming? How are decisions made concerning which persons will be in what groups? Who is involved in the decisions?

- Pray for the guidance of the Holy Spirit.

Prayer is important if the group is to be open to the movement of the Spirit and sensitive to the different feelings, attitudes, and ideas in the group. Provide time and a format for this prayer.

- Ask each member to share his or her position on the issue.

- Have members give all the "cons" of the issue. List the "cons" or reasons against such a proposal.

   "Cons" might include the following:

   • Our group has finally reached a level of trust where we can really challenge one another about important issues.

   • If we are always re-grouping, no group will ever have the chance to develop the full potential of a small Christian community, and such development is important for the church.

   • It has taken us so long to share prayer at a level of depth. This is now a very important and faith building part of our lives.

- Quietly reflect and pray over the "cons."

- Have members give all the "pros" of the issue. List the "pros" or reasons in support of the proposal.

   Pros might include the following:

- We've had very valuable experiences together. A new group could profit from our experiences. The core group is looking for leaders for these groups. Some of us could now provide this leadership.

- We might be getting too comfortable. Maybe we need new members in our group for our own growth.

- Somehow moving out to others seems to be more in line with the whole mission of the gospel.

– Quietly reflect and pray over the "pros."

– Open discussion. Are there clarifications, suggestions, new ideas, an integration of ideas?

For example, in response to the proposal someone might suggest that the present group expand and, in this way, involve additional parishioners in an experience of small Christian community.

Another suggestion might be to keep the groups intact, but to have the leaders of both experienced and new groups meet regularly in order to share experience and ideas.

– Check for possible consensus. Have each person state the position he or she can live with. The group might be ready to reach a consensus on this proposal at this point.

– If consensus is not reached at this point, re-evaluate the "pros" and "cons" lists, identify and con-

centrate on critical points, and try to integrate further the thinking of the group.

– Continue to encourage an atmosphere of optimism and mutual support.

Not to reach a decision is not an indictment of the group; it may simply indicate that a decision would be premature at this time. Those expressing genuine concerns should not be viewed as "blockers."

– When the leader feels that consensus has been reached, he or she should state the consensus that he or she thinks the group has reached and check with each member as to whether he or she can live with the statement. If he or she cannot, ask him or her if there are changes he or she could offer which would make the statement acceptable to him or her. Ask if the other members of the group can accept the changes.

– If consensus cannot be reached, the group may decide to table the issue. If a decision must be made, the group may have to come to an agreement on another method of making the decision.

– Thank God for the efforts and unity of the group in the process.

In the example proposal just presented, it would be important to celebrate whatever decision is reached—perhaps with a liturgy and a party. If the group has decided to re-group, it would be important to plan a special coming together in which the group could remember, reverence, celebrate, and laugh and cry over their times together.

SCRIPTURE SHARING (20 min.)

Ask for a volunteer to prepare the reading.

Leader: The following scripture reading is especially appropriate for this session on consensus.

Reading (Ephesians 4:1-6)

Questions for Discussion

How has decision-making in your small group/your parish been a source of unity?

How has decision-making in your small group/your parish been a source of disunity?

What specific attitudes and virtues would you like to develop more fully in yourself so that you can contribute more effectively to unity within your group/parish?

BUILDING UNDERSTANDING (5 min.)

Ask the participants to reflect on what other activities besides the six listed in Reflection Sheet #31 on page 67 of the Workbook prompt them to experience the closeness of God in their lives.

CLOSING PRAYER (5 min.)

Softly play the instrumental music used in the Opening Prayer. Ask the groups to pray the same verse
numbers they prayed during the Opening Prayer.

Leader: Let us quietly remember God's presence, a presence that
has been with us during all our discussion, sharing, and reflection
in this time we've been together.

(Pause for a few moments of reflection.)

Leader: Let us pray together.

1. O God, it is hard for me to let go,
        most times,
   and the squeeze I exert
        garbles me and gnarls others.
   So, loosen my grip a bit
        on the good times,
            on the moments of sunlight and star shine and joy,
   that the thousand graces they scatter as they pass
        may nurture growth in me
            rather than turn to brittle memories.

2. Loosen my grip
        on those grudges and grievances
            I hold so closely,
   that I may risk exposing myself
        to the spirit of forgiving and forgiveness
            that changes things and resurrects dreams and courage.

1. Loosen my grip
        on my fears
   that I may be released a little into humility
   and into an acceptance of my humanity.

2. Loosen my grip
        on myself
    that I may experience the freedom of a fool
            who knows that to believe
                    is to see kingdoms, find power, sense glory;
            to reach out
                    is to know myself held;
            to laugh at myself
                    is to be in on the joke of your grace;
    to attend to each moment
                    is to hear the faint melody of eternity;
            to dare love
                    is to smell the wild flowers of heaven.

1. Loosen my grip
    on my ways and words,
                    on my fears and fretfulness
    that letting go
            into the depths of silence
                    and my own uncharted longings,
    I may find myself held by you
            and linked anew to all life
                    in this wild and wondrous world
                            you love so much,
    so I may take to heart
            that you have taken me to heart.

From *Guerrillas of Grace*
by Ted Loder
LuraMedia, San Diego, CA, 1984

REFLECTION SHEET #29

Activities in Which "Core Catholics"
Experienced the Closeness of God

(An Individual Ranking)

A group of "Core Catholics"* were asked to rate activities which made them feel close to God. What follows are the activities that were listed. On the lines provided, rank these activities from 1 to 6 according to the way you think the activities were rated by the "Core Catholics." *Remember, you are ranking the items according to the way you think the "Core Catholics" ranked them*, not according to the way you would have ranked them. 1 will be the highest ranking; 6 will be the lowest.

____ Gathering with the congregation during Mass

____ Helping individuals in need

____ Obeying church rules

____ Being with a person I love

____ Receiving Holy Communion

____ Reading the gospels

*"Core Catholics" are defined as Catholics who are registered members of parishes. Some attended Mass regularly; some attended more sporadically. Some of these Catholics were actively involved in the parish as volunteers; some were not. This study included 2,667 Catholics from 36 parishes throughout the United States.

Taken from
The Emerging Parish: The Notre Dame Study of Catholic Life Since Vatican II
by Joseph Gremillion & Jim Castelli
Harper & Row, 1987

REFLECTION SHEET #30

Activities in Which "Core Catholics"
Experienced the Closeness of God

(A Consensus Ranking)

A group of "Core Catholics*" were asked to rate activities which made them feel close to God. What follows are the activities that were listed. On the lines provided, rank these activities from 1 to 6 according to the way you collectively think the activities were rated by the "Core Catholics." *Remember, you are ranking the items according to the way you think the "Core Catholics" ranked them,* not according to the way you would have ranked them. 1 will be the highest ranking; 6 will be the lowest.

___ Gathering with the congregation during Mass

___ Helping individuals in need

___ Obeying church rules

___ Being with a person I love

___ Receiving Holy Communion

___ Reading the gospels

*"Core Catholics" are defined as Catholics who are registered members of parishes. Some attended Mass regularly; some attended more sporadically. Some of these Catholics were actively involved in the parish as volunteers; some were not. This study included 2,667 Catholics from 36 parishes throughout the United States.

Taken from
The Emerging Parish: The Notre Dame Study of Catholic Life Since Vatican II
by Joseph Gremillion & Jim Castelli
Harper & Row, 1987

REFLECTION SHEET #31

**Activities in Which "Core Catholics"
Experienced the Closeness of God**

What follows are the rankings which "Core Catholics*" gave to experiences in which they felt the closeness of God:

_4_   Gathering with the congregation during Mass

_2_   Helping individuals in need

_6_   Obeying church rules

_3_   Being with a person I love

_1_   Receiving Holy Communion

_5_   Reading the gospels

*"Core Catholics" are defined as Catholics who are registered members of parishes. Some attended Mass regularly; some attended more sporadically. Some of these Catholics were actively involved in the parish as volunteers; some were not. This study included 2,667 Catholics from 36 parishes throughout the United States.

Taken from
*The Emerging Parish: The Notre Dame Study of
Catholic Life Since Vatican II*
by Joseph Gremillion & Jim Castelli
Harper & Row, 1987

MORE TIPS FOR LEADERS OF SMALL GROUPS

SAMPLE SCHEDULE

Welcome/Presentation of Aim	5 min.
Opening Prayer	5 min.
Group Experience, Part 1	20 min.
Presentation, Part 1	20 min.
Group Experience, Part 2	30 min.
Break	5 min.
Presentation, Part 2	5 min.
Scripture Sharing	20 min.
Building Understanding	5 min.
Closing Prayer	5 min.

PREPARATION

The Bible should be in a prominent position and opened to the reading from the book of Jeremiah which will be read during the Scripture Sharing segment.

AIM

To provide an opportunity—through group experience, discussion, presentation of information, prayer, and reflection—for participants to do the following:

- learn specific ways to help in the development of communities, especially in the area of sensitivity to persons, spirituality, vision, and a sense of celebration;
- review steps for good planning;
- assess some of their own leadership skills and attitudes.

WELCOME/PRESENTATION OF AIM (5 min.)

OPENING PRAYER (5 min.)

Call for Blessings

Leader: O God, we believe you love us and you want what is good for us and for those we love. We ask you to bless all those with whom we have shared community. We ask, especially, for your blessing on those with whom we are forming community at this time in our lives.

(Invite participants to name particular persons with whom they are in community and to ask for particular blessings for those persons. You may want to begin.)

Concluding Song

Leader: Let's conclude our prayer with a sense of peace and trust in the goodness and faithfulness of our God. Let's sing together "Peace Is Flowing Like a River."

GROUP EXPERIENCE, Part 1 (20 min.)

Explain to the participants that during this session they will be considering further aspects of leadership within the small community context. Tell them that they will not only have an opportunity to reflect on their own attitudes and feelings toward leadership but also will be able to further assess their strengths and weaknesses as leaders.

Ask them to take 5 or so minutes to reflect quietly on the following question.

Question for Reflection and Discussion

Think of a person you know who is an especially effective leader within small groups. What makes that person effective?

(Pause for a few minutes of reflection.)

After 5 or so minutes have passed, ask the participants to take approximately 15 minutes to share their reflections with their small group.

PRESENTATION OUTLINE, Part 1

I. Good leaders of small groups strive to be warm, open, friendly, sensitive, and enthusiastic.

II. Good small group leadership requires sensitivity to people.
   A. This sensitivity includes the virtue of hospitality which involves concrete details including the following:
      1. room arrangement
      2. creating environment
      3. organizing refreshments
      4. limiting distractions
      5. welcoming people
      6. follow-up on absentees
   B. Sensitivity to people includes a positive attitude of believing in and caring about people which is shown by the following:
      1. encouraging others, especially those who are shy and unsure
      2. supporting all group members
      3. challenging the group to greater commitment, honesty and authenticity
      4. encouraging members to acknowledge and use their gifts
      5. being aware of and concerned about the joys, sorrows, and problems in members' lives
      6. being positive about the ability of the group to grow
      7. being willing to share one's own problems, struggles, and pain
      8. admitting limitations and mistakes

III. Good small group leadership requires a concern for one's own spirituality and the spirituality of the group. Such concern includes the following:
   A. personal efforts to grow spiritually
   B. regular prayer
   C. introducing varied prayer forms to the group
   D. suggesting days of recollection, retreats, educational opportunities, and spiritual reading materials to the group

E.   encouraging the group to participate in the spiritual life of the parish

F.   being willing to share one's experience of God in his or her own life, as well as personal efforts to live a Christian life, and to pray; encouraging this same kind of sharing within the group

G.   urging group members to take responsibility for spiritual growth

IV.   Good small group leadership requires a wide vision which can be encouraged in the members by the following:

A.   calling attention to the activities and ministries of the parish, the diocese, and the universal church and encouraging participation in such activities and ministries

B.   pointing out the importance of small Christian communities in the church

C.   stressing the importance of outreach and service

D.   encouraging the group to become more aware of the church's social teaching and specific social concerns

E.   including a variety of concerns in the course of prayer and reflection

F.   urging the group to see the connections between their spiritual growth and the growth and well-being of the church, society, and the whole of creation

V.   Good small group leadership requires a sense of celebration, including suggestions of celebratory and festive activities for the group to enjoy, such as the following:

A.   holiday celebrations

B.   involvement of the families in some group activities

C.   celebration of members' birthdays and other important life events

PRESENTATION, Part 1 (20 min.)

In past sessions, we have discussed the nature of small groups and the variety of communication skills necessary if small groups are to develop into caring communities. In this session, we will be talking about other concrete ways in which leaders can help their small groups to grow and mature. You will have an opportunity to assess your own strengths and weaknesses in relationship to these aspects of leadership.

A good small group leader is warm, open, friendly, sensitive, and enthusiastic. While avoiding any inclination to be overly controlling, this leader does strive to create a climate of understanding and acceptance. The leader is not the "expert," but rather freely acknowledges personal limitations and welcomes new information, ideas, and insights.

What follows are some concrete suggestions for group leaders. These suggestions are grouped in four categories: sensitivity to people, spirituality, wider vision, and a sense of celebration. While the leaders themselves may not actually undertake all the tasks listed, they are aware of these tasks and make sure that some member of the group is attentive to them.

Sensitivity to People

A good small group leader knows the importance of the virtue of hospitality and so is concerned about the following:

- the arrangement of the room: it is important that individuals can see and hear one another clearly. Placing chairs in a circle can help communication.

- creating an environment: the use of candles (and other symbols, for example, the Bible enthroned), music, pictures (slides, photos), etc., can do much to create a prayerful, reflective atmosphere. This requires planning, however.

- the organization of refreshments: a common understanding that refreshments are ordinarily to be simple is important for the groups and avoids the danger of members trying to "outdo" one another. (It may be decided that different members will bring the refreshments each week.) Serving refreshments during the meeting can be distracting; it is worth the time to determine, with the group, what the policy with regard to refreshments will be.

- limiting distractions: for example, a noisy television or a constantly ringing telephone negatively affects the environment.

- providing a sense of welcome, especially to new members: for example, making sure that they are introduced to everyone.

- following up on absent members with a phone call or a visit to let them know they were missed: for example, checking on difficulties such as transportation (providing a ride if necessary).

A good small group leader believes in people, cares about them, and shows it in a variety of ways including the following:

SENSITIVITY

- ENCOURAGING OTHERS, ESPECIALLY SHY AND UNSURE PEOPLE

- SUPPORTING ALL

- CHALLENGING THE GROUP TO COMMITMENT AND HONESTY

- ENCOURAGING OTHERS TO USE GIFTS

- BEING AWARE OF JOYS, SORROWS, PROBLEMS

- BEING POSITIVE ABOUT GROWTH

- BEING WILLING TO SHARE OWN PROBLEMS, STRUGGLES, PAIN

- ADMITTING LIMITATIONS AND MISTAKES

- encouraging those who may be shy and unsure of themselves. During the meeting it is sometimes helpful to ask quiet members if they would like to share their ideas with the group. If there seems to be hesitancy, the leader might speak to the individual over refreshments, asking for his or her reactions to the sharing.

- supporting all group members and finding good even in those to whom the leader would not naturally gravitate.

- challenging the group to greater honesty, commitment, and authenticity.

- encouraging members to acknowledge and use their gifts and talents, urging members to minister to others in and beyond the group.

- being aware of and concerned about joys, sorrows, and problems in the lives of individual members and encouraging the group to be supportive at such times. The birth of a child, sickness, and death in the family are events in which the group can share, offering loving, practical help. Some such situations may call for a special sensitivity. For example, a member who has lost his or her job may be embarrassed and suffering a lessening of self-esteem. In such a case, the leader could speak to the individual privately, offering support and also encouraging the member to trust enough to share the problem with the group.

- being positive about the ability of the group to mature, manage difficulties, solve problems, and grow through their experiences together.

- being willing to share one's own pain, problems, and struggles with the group. Part of caring for others is allowing them to care for us.

- admitting limitations and mistakes. The leader can encourage honesty and openness in the group by his or her own forthrightness and willingness to acknowledge personal strengths and failures.

Spirituality

A good small group leader nurtures the spiritual growth of the community. What follows are some practical suggestions of ways in which the leader can do this:

- A concern for prayer, reflection, spiritual reading, and education must mark the personal life of the leader since the leader is called to encourage the members in these areas.

- Praying regularly for the group and each of its members is an excellent spiritual commitment to the community.

- The leader can introduce different prayer forms for the group and for individual members. For some, spiritual direction will be an attractive possibility.

- The leader can suggest evenings or days of recollection, retreat experiences, educational opportunities, and spiritual reading material for the group and for individual members. The parish staff can be an excellent resource in these areas.

- The parish often offers a variety of opportunities for spiritual growth. In the parish, the members participate in the eucharist and in the total sacramental life of the church. The leader can encourage individual members or the group as a whole to view sacramental life as an expression of Christian spirituality and as fundamental to being church, the body of Christ.

- The leader's willingness to share how faith has affected his or her life, his or her understanding of God's action in life, and personal efforts to be faithful to the gospel will encourage other members to do likewise.

- The leader can urge all members to take responsibility for spiritual growth, to share resources with one another, and to challenge the group to a deeper spiritual life.

Encouraging a WIDE VISION

- ○ PARTICIPATION IN PARISH, DIOCESE, UNIVERSAL CHURCH
- ○ IMPORTANCE OF SCCs
- ○ OUTREACH AND SERVICE
- ○ CHURCH'S SOCIAL TEACHING
- ○ VARIETY OF CONCERNS IN PRAYER AND EDUCATION
- ○ CONNECTIONS BETWEEN OWN SPIRITUAL GROWTH AND THE GROWTH AND WELL-BEING OF CHURCH, SOCIETY AND WHOLE OF CREATION

The continued life, authenticity, and vitality of the community require that the group look beyond itself. The leader can facilitate this outward vision in the following ways:

- by calling attention to the activities of the parish, the diocese, and the universal church.

- by pointing out the importance and potential in the development of small communities within the parish and the wider church.

- by stressing the importance of the outreach and service of the group and its individual members.

- by encouraging and helping the group to become more aware of the social teaching of the church and specific social concerns through discussion, reading, and educational opportunities. People who are knowledgeable in specific issues and concerns could be invited to speak with the group.

- by including a wide variety of concerns in the course of the prayer, reflection, and education of the community.

- by consistently urging the group to see the connections between their own personal growth, development, and integrity and that of the group, the church, the society, and the whole of creation.

Sense of Celebration

A group will grow in its sense of bondedness if, at least sometimes, the members share socially and experience this form of celebration together. The leader could encourage such sharing through suggestions such as the following:

- holiday celebrations (for example, Christmas, Easter, July 4) which could include family members' families

- involvement of members' families in special activities; for example, outreach actions, special prayer experiences, and socials like picnics, parties, and camping weekends

- celebrations of members' birthdays and special events in their lives; for example, engagements, weddings, graduations, and baptisms of children.

GROUP EXPERIENCE, Part 2 (30 min.)

Explain that this Group Experience will provide participants with an opportunity to assess some aspects of their leadership. Have participants turn to Reflection Sheet #32 on page 76 of their Workbooks. Ask them to take 10 minutes or so to complete Reflection Sheet #32. Have the participants conclude this segment in about 20 minutes of discussion as follows.

> After you complete Reflection Sheet #32, discuss within your small group your reflections on your contributions to small groups and on the difficulty and ease with which you contributed to these groups in terms of sensitivity to people, spirituality, wider vision, and a sense of celebration.

BREAK (5 min.)

PRESENTATION OUTLINE, Part 2

VI. In planning projects, programs, and activities it is helpful for the small group to be familiar with basic questions important for effective planning. These questions include the following:
   A. Why?
   B. Who?
   C. What?
   D. Where?
   E. When?
   F. How?
   G. How evaluated?

PRESENTATION, Part 2 (5 min.)

All small groups, at some time, are involved in some specific planning, perhaps, for a particular activity, program, or project. While most people have some experience in planning events and projects (within their family or work situations), it is helpful to have a clear idea of the points that should be included as they plan. The questions in Reflection Sheet #33 found on pages 77-78 of the Workbook can assure individuals and small groups, and especially those responsible for leadership, that such points are being covered. If we use the example of a small group deciding to undertake a project, we can consider these questions:

Why?

Are all members of the group clear on why the group has decided to do the project and how this project fits in with the life and purpose of the group?

Who?

Who is doing the project and for whom is the project being done or to whom is it directed? It is important that the group be very clear on which members have specific responsibilities in the project. It is helpful to keep a written record of these responsibilities.

What?

Is everyone clear on the exact nature and content of the project?

Where?

What are the location and environment of the project?

When?

What is the schedule for the project? It is often helpful to develop a timeline which shows what tasks related to the project have to be done and when each task will be completed.

How?

The "how" question is answered by an overview of the project which includes steps to be taken, tasks to be done, persons responsible for the tasks, and the resources needed to accomplish the tasks.

How evaluated?

The group should determine how and when the project will be evaluated. Questions for evaluation would include: Did the project achieve its goals? Was the group faithful to tasks and timeline?

SCRIPTURE SHARING (20 min.)

Ask for a volunteer to prepare the scripture reading.

Reading (Jeremiah 1:4-10)

After the reading is completed, ask the participants to discuss the following questions.

Questions for Discussion

Jeremiah was afraid when the Lord called him to leadership. What fears do you have when you are called to leadership? What specific graces do you request when you ask God to help you to lead effectively?

BUILDING UNDERSTANDING (5 min.)

Ask the participants to reflect on what points covered during this session could help them overcome the difficulty they perceive in their handling of one of the following in a small group situation: sensitivity to people in the group, spirituality, wider vision, or sense of celebration.

CLOSING PRAYER (5 min.)

Play soft instrumental music throughout the Closing Prayer.

Call to Quiet

Leader: Let us quiet ourselves and remember that we are in the presence of God.

(Pause for a moment of reflection.)

Leader: We ask for God's blessings as we minister within our small communities.

All: God, our Creator and Source of life and growth, give us the gifts we need to minister well in our small communities. Strengthen our trust in you, as we strive to be witnesses to our brother, Jesus, in all that we do. We ask you, especially, for the following blessings.

Leader: For the gift of faithfulness,

All: to live your call to build up our world and to serve our sisters and brothers with love.

Leader: For the gift of sensitivity,

All: that we may empty ourselves enough to know the joys and sorrows of others.

Leader: For the gift of honesty,

All: to see things as they really are.

Leader: For the gift of patience,

All: to wait for the fullness of your reign coming to birth in ourselves and others.

Leader: For the gift of enthusiasm,

All: to believe in great possibilities that your presence and power can bring forth in ourselves, in others, and in your world.

Leader: For the gift of gentleness,

All: to stand in profound respect of the uniqueness of every person.

Leader: For the gift of vision,

All: that we may see beyond ourselves and believe that our small efforts can affect the universe.

Leader: For the gift of encouragement,

All: that we may affirm the gifts of others and not see them as threats to ourselves.

Leader: For the gift of celebration,

All: that we may rejoice in the countless ways in which you lavish your love upon us. We ask you, God, for these blessings, confident in your constant care. Amen.

REFLECTION SHEET #32

Assessing Aspects of Leadership

Consider groups of which you have been a part. Consider groups
in which you have been the leader. Using the categories listed
below, list specific ways in which you contributed to these aspects
of the groups' life and growth.

Sensitivity to People

Spirituality

Wider Vision

Sense of Celebration

Considering the preceding categories, in which area do you find it
most difficult to help in a group? Why do you find it difficult? In
which area do you find it easiest to help in a group? Why do you
find it easy?

REFLECTION SHEET #33

Questions in Planning

Why?   Why is the group doing the project? How does
                        it fit in with the purpose and life of the group?

Who?   Who is doing the project? For whom is the proj-
                        ect being done? To whom is the project directed?

What?   What are the nature and content of the project?

Where?   What are the location and environment of the
                        project?

When?   What are the schedule and timeline for the pro-
                        ject and the tasks related to it?

How?   Is there an overview of the project which
                        includes steps to be taken, tasks to be done, per-
                        sons responsible, and resources needed to
                        accomplish the tasks?

How evaluated?   How and when will the project be evaluated?
                        Questions to be asked include: Did the project
                        achieve its goals? Was the group faithful to its
                        tasks and timeline?

LIFE IN A SMALL GROUP— WHAT'S DIFFICULT FOR ME?

SAMPLE SCHEDULE

Welcome/Presentation of Aim	5 min.
Opening Prayer	5 min.
Group Exercise	75 min.
Break	5 min.
Scripture Sharing	20 min.
Building Understanding	5 min.
Closing Prayer	5 min.

PREPARATION

The Bible should be displayed prominently, opened to the verse from the book of Isaiah from which part of the Opening Prayer is taken.

When the participants have formed their small groups, designate which groups will pray the verses indicated with a "1." and which will pray the verses indicated with a "2."

AIM

To provide an opportunity—through group experience, discussion, reflection, and prayer—for participants to do the following:

- assess some of their own strengths and weaknesses in participating in and leading small groups;
- gain confidence in areas of weakness by considering their hopes and fears relative to these areas.

WELCOME/PRESENTATION OF AIM (5 min.)

OPENING PRAYER (5 min.)

Call to Awareness

Leader: Let us begin by opening our awareness to the presence of God's Spirit in our midst.

(short pause)

Leader: The Spirit of the Lord is a spirit of wisdom and insight, a spirit of counsel and power, a spirit of knowledge and of holy fear (Is 11:2).

1. We worship you, Holy Spirit of God,
   and we may only guess, as best we can,
   who you are for us.

2. We open our hearts to receive you
   that we may learn
   how deeply and invisibly you are present everywhere.

1. You are the air we breathe,
   the distance we gaze into,
   the space that surrounds us.
   You are the kindly light
   in which people are attractive to each other.

2. You are the finger of God
   with which God playfully ordered the universe.
   You are the sensitive love with which God created us.

1. We pray to you, Spirit of God, Creator,
   complete the work you have begun,
   prevent the evil we are capable of doing
   and inspire us toward what is good.

2. To faithfulness and patience,
   to compassion and gentleness,
   and awaken in us friendship for every living being
   with joy for everything that is good and human.

1. Everything that lives, grows only by your power.
   Your activity is strange and beyond all human words.
   You are hidden deep inside us
   like yeast, a seed of fire.

2. You are our will to live,
   the love that keeps us here on earth
   and ties us to our God.

1. You urge us to go on to the end
   and to endure everything,
   not to give way but to go on hoping,
   as love does.

2. You are the soul of all our prayers
    so there is nothing we may not expect from you—
    wisdom to understand each other,
    readiness to help each other…

1. You are God's gift to us.
    Be present here among us, then,
    God in us.

2. Glory to the Creator, who brings us into being,
    to the Son, who has redeemed us,
    and to the Spirit, who is the life of Divinity within us.

All: As it was in the beginning, is now, and ever shall be. Amen.

Source Unknown

GROUP EXPERIENCE (75 min.)

Leader: In the past eight sessions, we have explored several important aspects of facilitating a small group. Leadership within such groups requires commitment, skill, and often, a willingness to sacrifice one's own comfort level and sense of security in certain behavior patterns. Personal and group growth and maturing will involve some risks. Leaders can gain valuable insights by exploring challenges that may be particularly difficult for them as they try to assist their groups in this growth process. In this session, we will have the opportunity to reflect on and discuss some of these challenges. We'll start by completing the exercise on Reflection Sheet #34 on pages 84-86 of the Workbook.

It should take about 10 minutes for the participants to complete Reflection Sheet #34. After 10 or so minutes, when it seems that the participants have completed the exercise, ask them to discuss the following questions in their small groups.

Questions for Discussion

Review the statements that have a minus mark. Although these actions were difficult for you, what helped you to do them effectively?

Review statements marked "0." When are these actions easy for you? When are they difficult?

Share with the group those actions that you find easy or very easy to do. Why are they easy for you?

This part of the exercise should take about 20 minutes. After 20 or so minutes, when it seems that the participants have finished their discussions, ask the participants to complete on their own Reflection Sheet #35 on pages 87-90 of the Workbook. Let them know that they will have approximately 20 minutes for this segment.

After 20 minutes or so, invite the participants to take about 25 minutes to share within their group the responses to the questions posed in Reflection Sheet #35.

BREAK (5 min.)

SCRIPTURE SHARING (20 min.)

Ask for a volunteer to prepare the reading.

Reading (John 12:24-25)

Invite the participants to share, in an orderly fashion,
their reflections on the following questions.

Questions for Discussion

Describe some specific leaders and how, in giving of themselves
for the good of the community, they brought new life to those
communities.

What virtues did Jesus teach that are most needed for good leadership in our world today?

BUILDING UNDERSTANDING (5 min.)

Ask participants to reflect on the one facet of their
personality that they learned about most while working on the Reflection Sheets for this session.

CLOSING PRAYER (5 min.)

Ask for four volunteers to prepare the readings and to read slowly, allowing for a brief pause after each reading.

Call to Listen

Leader: For our Closing Prayer, we will simply listen reflectively to some short scripture passages, pausing between each passage. Let us begin by closing our eyes, breathing deeply and, in a relaxed and peaceful manner, opening our minds and hearts to the Word of God.

(brief pause)

Reading 1 (Matthew 5:13-14)

(pause)

Reading 2 (Matthew 11:28-30)

(pause)

Reading 3 (John 14:16-17)

(pause)

Reading 4 (John 15:12-13)

(pause)

Concluding Prayer

All: We thank God, in our hearts, for the call to leadership and for the blessing of strength to answer that call.

REFLECTION SHEET #34

Some Challenges for Members of Small Groups

1. Considering your actions in groups of which you have been a member, rate the following statements on the basis of how difficult the actions are for you to do. Write the appropriate number from the scale below in front of each item.

very difficult for me	difficult for me	I have no feelings one way or another; I don't know	easy for me	very easy for me
___ -2 _____	-1 _____	0 _____	+1 _____	+2 ___

____ 1. making a statement which might anger someone else in the group

____ 2. expressing and dealing with a conflict that I have with another member of the group

____ 3. acknowledging my strengths and talents in the group

____ 4. naming a conflict that the group has been avoiding or denying

____ 5. praying spontaneously during the prayer segment of the meeting

____ 6. sharing my personal life and experiences in the group

____ 7. sharing my understanding of God in the group

____ 8. expressing my needs and wants in a conflict

____ 9. believing that everyone involved in a conflict in the group is basically of good will

___ 10. listening carefully, dispassionately, and objectively to the "cons" position on an issue when I am strongly supportive of the "pros" position

___ 11. asking for help with my problems from others in the group

___ 12. asking for feedback from members of the group

___ 13. challenging a group to develop in areas in which they seem less interested (for example, learning, outreach, shared prayer)

___ 14. giving another member positive feedback

___ 15. giving another member negative feedback

___ 16. being the center of attention in the group

___ 17. expressing confusion and uncertainty in front of the group

___ 18. admitting that I was wrong about some other person in the group

___ 19. admitting to the group that I was wrong about an idea that I had

___ 20. admitting that someone in the group had hurt my feelings

___ 21. asking members of the group to assume responsibilities and to take on tasks in the group

2. Review those statements marked "-2" or "-1." Place a check next to those statements marked "-2" or "-1" that describe actions that are difficult for you, but that you have done effectively.

(This exercise is adapted from *A Handbook of Structured Experiences for Human Relations Training,* Vol. 4, ed. by J. William Pfeiffer & John E. Jones, University Associates Publishers and Consultants, La Jolla, California, 1974.)

REFLECTION SHEET #35

Considering Behavior That Is Difficult for You

Choose the three statements that describe behavior that would be most difficult for you, as indicated on Reflection Sheet #34. Write those statements in the column on the left. In the column on the right, write what you think would be the worst thing that could happen if you tried this behavior and what would be the best thing that could happen if you tried this behavior. When you have completed this section, answer the question at the end of this Reflection Sheet.

Your first statement:

What is the worst thing that could happen if you tried this behavior?

What is the best thing that could happen if you tried this behavior?

Your second statement:

What is the worst thing
that could happen if you
tried this behavior?

What is the best thing
that could happen if you
tried this behavior?

Your third statement:

What is the worst thing that could happen if you tried this behavior?

What is the best thing that could happen if you tried this behavior?

Describe an experience in which you tried one of the preceding behaviors within a small group setting. What were the results?

A REFLECTION ON BEING CALLED

SAMPLE SCHEDULE

Welcome/Presentation of Aim	5 min.
Opening Prayer	20 min.
Group Reflection	45 min.
Closing Prayer	20 min.
Socializing/Celebration	

AIM

To provide an opportunity—through reflection, discussion, prayer, and socializing—for participants to do the following:

- come to a greater understanding of God's call in their lives;
- indicate a willingness to respond to that call;
- celebrate with one another.

PREPARATION

This final session will combine reflection, sharing, and a singular sense of celebration. Special touches such as a bouquet of flowers, a festive candle, soft lights, specially prepared refreshments, etc., will help to create the celebratory atmosphere of this session. There will be a reduction of the usual two-hour format of scheduled activity to one-and-a-half hours to allow an extended period for socializing and celebrating.

The Bible should be positioned prominently and opened to the verse from the letter to the Romans which is included in the Opening Prayer.

Ask for two volunteers to prepare the readings for the Opening Prayer. Tell them that they will alternate the passages they read and encourage them to read the verses slowly.

WELCOME/PRESENTATION OF AIM (5 min.)

OPENING PRAYER (20 min.)

Leader: In this last session we will be spending more time in reflection, in prayer, and in celebrating our experience of growing together during these leadership development sessions.

It is an opportunity to pause, to become more aware of God's presence, and to review how the Spirit has been acting in our personal histories, bringing us to this moment when we are called to be members and leaders in small Christian communities.

Call to Quiet and Relaxation

Leader: Let us begin by quieting ourselves and relaxing in God's presence.

(Read the following very slowly.)

Take up a posture that is comfortable and restful. Close your eyes. Become aware of what your body is feeling at this particular moment. Be aware of the touch of your clothes on your back...on your shoulders...on your arms...on your legs. Feel your back touching the back of the chair on which you are sitting....Be aware of the feel of your hands as they touch each other or rest on your lap....Feel your feet touching your shoes...the hardness of the floor on which your feet are resting.

Again, take a few seconds to be aware of your shoulders...now your head...your left hand...your right hand...your neck...your chest...your stomach...your thighs.

Continue to go the round by yourself now, moving from one part of your body to another.

Spend a few seconds on each part. Then move to another part. Do this quietly, yourself, for several minutes.

> Adapted from
> *Sadhana, A Way to God*
> by Anthony de Mello
> Image Books, A Division
> of Doubleday & Co., Inc.
> Garden City, NY, 1984

(Allow 2-3 minutes of silence.)

Leader: Now, remaining relaxed, let us listen to the following passages from the Word of God.

Readings

Reader 1: You did not choose me, but I chose you and appointed you that you should go and bear fruit and that your fruit should abide; so that whatever you ask God in my name, God may give it to you (Jn 15:16).

Reader 2: Hear me, O coastlands, listen, O distant peoples. God called me from birth, from my mother's womb God pronounced my name.

He made of me a sharp-edged sword and concealed me in the shadow of his arm. He made me a polished arrow, in his quiver he hid me. You are my servant, he said to me, Israel, through whom I show my glory (Is 49:1-3).

Reader 1: Fear not, for I have redeemed you; I have called you by name: you are mine (Is 43:1b).

Reader 2: As he was walking by the Sea of Galilee, he saw two brothers, Simon who is called Peter and his brother Andrew. He said to them, "Come after me." He walked along from there and saw two other brothers, James, the son of Zebedee, and his brother John. He called them (Mt. 4:18a, 19a, 21).

Reader 1: For the gifts and the call of God are irrevocable (Rom 11: 29).

Reader 2: May the eyes of [your] hearts be enlightened, that you may know what is the hope that belongs to his call, what are the riches of glory in his inheritance among the holy ones, and what is the surpassing greatness of his power for us who believe, in accord with the exercise of his great might (Eph 1:18-19).

Leader: Our God has called us into being and continually calls us to new life. God calls us through all the circumstances of our life. God calls us now to leadership in our small groups—leadership in the Christian community. Let us prayerfully reflect on God's call in our lives. I invite you to speak a word or a phrase that swells within you as you think of God's call to you.

(You may want to start by speaking a word or phrase.)

Leader: Our God calls us to be leaders of small Christian communities. Sometimes, we are fearful. We have self-doubts. We want to stay secure and avoid mistakes. Sometimes, we are weary and resist the call to leadership because it takes too much effort. I invite you, prayerfully, to name your fears and hesitations and to place them before God.

(You may want to start by naming a fear or hesitation.)

Leader: Our God says, "Do not be afraid, for I have redeemed you. I have called you by name, you are mine." God promises constant help and support to strengthen us in our leadership responsibilities. God will always answer us when we ask for those blessings we need to be good leaders. I invite you now to name the blessing or gift for which you pray.

(You may want to start by naming a blessing or gift.)

Concluding Song

Leader: In thanksgiving for the gift of God's call, let us sing together "Amazing Grace."

GROUP REFLECTION (45 min.)

Leader: The events and people, the thoughts and feelings which make up our lives are steppingstones which are meant to lead us along a path which guides us into an ever fuller and deeper relationship with God and with one another. Your call to life and leadership in your small group is the result of a history of circumstances which have brought you to this moment. In retrospect, we can often see how God was calling us to growth and to a greater fullness of life through particular situations.

Have participants turn to Reflection Sheet #36 on pages 96-97 of their Workbooks. Ask them to take 20 minutes or so to complete Reflection Sheet #36. Have the participants conclude this segment in about 25 minutes of sharing as follows.

After you complete Reflection Sheet #36, share the answers to the following questions with your small group, being conscious of the importance of each person's contribution and allowing enough time for each person to share personal reflections.

Questions for Sharing

What talents, qualities, skills, and gifts have you developed because of your involvement and responsibilities in communities?

What events, persons, and ideas stood out as you completed Reflection Sheet #36?

CLOSING PRAYER (20 min.)

A small dish of baby oil will be needed for the Closing Prayer.

Leader: We have completed many sessions in which we have come to a better understanding of membership and leadership in a small Christian community. We end this time we have spent together by sending forth one another to participate in the realization of God's reign through the building up of the Christian community. Let us begin with an act of faith.

It is an act of uncommon courage to make a public affirmation of faith. For some, such an act may mean their lives. For us, it is only words in prayer and worship. But if we begin to hear and live out these words, it will mean our lives too. Let us dare to affirm our faith.

Act of Faith

All: We believe in God, the creator of heaven and earth.

We believe in Jesus Christ, God's only Son, our Lord.

We believe that Jesus was conceived by the power of the Holy Spirit and born of Mary.
We believe that he was crucified, died, and was buried.
We believe that Jesus rose from the dead.

We believe in the Holy Spirit, the holy catholic church, the communion of saints, the forgiveness of sins, the resurrection of the body, and life everlasting.

Leader: I invite you, in your own words, to mention a specific Christian belief that gives special meaning and purpose to your life.

(It will be helpful if you start with a short and simple statement of belief.)

Leader: Let us listen to the word of God.

Reading (John 15:16-17)

Leader: We will send forth one another by an anointing with oil. Anointing with oil is an ancient custom. Throughout history, kings and queens, soldiers, and those in need of special strength have been anointed. In the sacramental life of the church, blessed oil is used in baptism, confirmation, and ordination. Oil symbolizes strength, healing, gladness, and compassion. In preparation for anointing, let us voice, together, our intention to be faithful to God's call.

Faithfulness to God's Call

All: Christ Jesus, whose death and resurrection we remember and whose second coming we await…with your help we will do our best
> To say the word,
> And do the work,
> And be the person
> In whom our neighbors may see
> God's reign coming near
> And God's holy love revealed.

Leader: Jesus accepts our honest intentions, and will give us the help we need to perform them faithfully.

All: God help us to do so.

Leader: I'll now go from person to person with this oil. Each person is invited to dip a finger in the oil and then to trace the sign of the cross on the forehead of the person to his or her right, saying "I anoint you with oil and urge you to live out your Christian commitment with a generous heart."

Anointing

Kiss of Peace

Leader: Let us now exchange the kiss of peace with one another.

Concluding Song

Leader: Let us conclude by singing "City of God."

Excerpts from Closing Prayer adapted from
Women and Worship
by Sharon Neufer Emswiler
Thomas Neufer Emswiler
Harper & Row, NY, 1984

REFLECTION SHEET #36

Reflection on My Life

The events and people, the thoughts and feelings which make up our lives are steppingstones which are meant to lead us along a path which guides us into an ever fuller and deeper relationship with God and with one another. Your call to life and leadership in your small group is the result of a history of circumstances which have brought you to this moment. God has been working through these circumstances. In retrospect, we can often see how God was calling us to growth and to a greater fullness of life through particular situations.

Think back on your life and, in the space below each item, write down the events/circumstances, people, and ideas through which you came to a greater appreciation of the importance of community in your life, through which God called you to involvement and responsibility in community, and through which you came to realize that you have gifts and talents to share with the community.

Events/Circumstances

People

Ideas

What specific talents, skills, and gifts have you come to recognize
and develop because of the events, persons, and ideas mentioned
above?

MUSIC RESOURCES

Session 25
Instrumental Music

Session 29
"Spirit of the Living God," Album: *Song of Praise*, Vol. 1, Sparrow Corp.

Session 30
"Let There Be Peace on Earth," Album: *Gather to Remember*, Miller/Jackson, G.I.A.

Session 31
Instrumental Music

Session 32
"Peace Is Flowing Like a River," Album: *Glory and Praise*, Vol. 1, Cary Landry, NALR.
Instrumental Music

Session 34
"City of God," Album: *Glory and Praise*, Vol. 3, Dan Schutte, S.J., NALR.

SUGGESTIONS FOR INSTRUMENTAL MUSIC

The Fairy Ring, Mike Rowland, Nevada Distributing, 207 E. Buffalo, Milwaukee, WI 53202.

Meditation, Contemplative Moments in Music, Polygram Classics, Inc., 137 W. 55 St., New York, NY 10017.

Play Before God, G.I.A.

Reflections, Vol. 3., Instrumental Music by the Dameans, NALR.

Solitude, Zamfir, Polygram Classics, Inc., 137 W. 55 St., New York, NY 10017.

Waiting Moments, Gregory Norbet, OCP Publications, 5536 NE Hassalo, Portland, OR 97213.

PUBLISHERS' ADDRESSES

G.I.A. Publications, Inc., 7404 S. Mason Ave., Chicago, IL 60638.

North American Liturgy Resources (NALR), 2110 W. Peoria, Phoenix, AZ 85029.

Sparrow Corp., Box 5010, Brentwood, TN 37024-5010.

BIBLIOGRAPHY

GENERAL REFERENCES

The following church documents are general references used in the development of all 34 sessions. Some are also specifically cited in particular sessions.

Documents of Vatican II

Lumen gentium: Dogmatic Constitution on the Church (*LG*).

Dei Verbum: Dogmatic Constitution on Divine Revelation (*DV*).

Sacrosanctum concilium: Constitution on the Sacred Liturgy (*SC*).

Gaudium et spes: Pastoral Constitution on the Church in the Modern World (*GS*).

Apostolicam actuositatem: Decree on the Apostolate of the Laity (*AA*).

Presbyterorum ordinis: Decree on the Ministry and Life of Priests (*PO*).

Gravissimum educationis: Declaration on Christian Education (*GE*).

Other Church Documents

John Paul II. *Laborem Exercens:* On Human Work, 1981.

_____. *Christifidelis Laici:* The Vocation and Mission of the Lay Faithful in the Church in the World, 1988.

United States Catholic Conference. *Economic Justice for All: Catholic Social Teaching and the U.S. Economy.* United States Bishops, 1986.

Additional General Resources

Brown, Raymond, E., S.S., Fitzmyer, Joseph, A., S.J., and Murphy, Roland E., O. Carm., eds. *The New Jerome Biblical Commentary.* Englewood Cliffs, NJ: Prentice Hall, 1990.

Libreria Editrice Vaticana, *Catechism of the Catholic Church.* Mahwah, NJ: Paulist Press et al., proximate.

Sharing the Light of Faith: National Catechetical Directory for Catholics of the United States. Washington, DC: United States Catholic Conference Department of Education, 1979.

SPECIFIC REFERENCES ON GROUP DEVELOPMENT

Keating, Charles J. *The Leadership Book: Revised.* Mahwah, NJ: Paulist Press, 1982.

Lawyer, John W., and Katz, Neil H. *Communication Skills for Ministry.* Dubuque, IA: Kendall/Hunt Publishing Co., 1983.

Napier, Rodney W., and Gershenfeld, Matti K. *Groups: Theory and Experience.* Boston: Houghton Mifflin Co., 1981.

Pfeiffer, J. William, and Jones, John E. *A Handbook of Structured Experiences for Human Relations Training.* La Jolla, CA: University Associates Publishers and Consultants, 1974.

Sofield, Loughlan, S.T., and Juliano, Carroll, S.H.C.J. *Collaborative Ministry: Skills and Guidelines.* Notre Dame, IN: Ave Maria Press, 1987.

NOTES

NOTES

NOTES